The Penguin Book of
# Canadian Biography
# for Young Readers
# Early Canada

Pat Hancock

**VIKING**

VIKING

Published by the Penguin Group

Penguin Books Canada Ltd, 10 Alcorn Avenue, Toronto, Ontario,
Canada M4V 3B2

Penguin Books Ltd, 27 Wrights Lane, London W8 5TZ, England

Penguin Putnam Inc., 375 Hudson Street, New York, New York 10014, U.S.A.

Penguin Books Australia Ltd, Ringwood, Victoria, Australia

Penguin Books (NZ) Ltd, cnr Rosedale and Airborne Roads, Albany,
Auckland 1310, New Zealand

Penguin Books Ltd, Registered Offices: Harmondsworth, Middlesex, England

First published 1999

1   3   5   7   9   10   8   6   4   2

Printed and bound in Canada on acid-free paper  ⊛

CANADIAN CATALOGUING IN PUBLICATION DATA

Hancock, Pat
The Penguin book of Canadian biography for young readers: early Canada

ISBN 0-670-88600-9

1. Canada – Biography – Juvenile literature.   I. Title.

FC25.H36 1999     j971'.000'9     C99-931273-1
F1005.H36 1999

Visit Penguin Canada's Website at www.penguin.ca

*To Madeline,*
*for her inspiration,*
*and to Claire,*
*for her example and support*

# Acknowledgements

I WANT TO THANK Joanne Cosgrove for coming up with the idea for this book, and Loretta McCloskey-Mackenzie for passing that idea along to Penguin's editors.

I would also like to acknowledge the invaluable resources to be found within the twelve volumes of the *Dictionary of Canadian Biography*, published by University of Toronto Press. I often turned to these books to cross-check information and, in some cases, look for details not readily available in other sources.

Thanks, too, to my son, Michael, who organized my many computer files; to my husband, Ron, for his patient support; and to my friend, Dyanne Rivers, who always lent a sympathetic ear when I needed to rant on about finding conflicting information.

# Contents

# Introduction

A COUNTRY'S HISTORY is like a magnificent tapestry woven from the threads of its people's lives. Most of these threads blend into each other. That doesn't mean, however, that they aren't important. They are what holds the tapestry together and keeps it strong. But some colourful threads really stand out, and these give shape to the tapestry's overall picture or design. This book is about a few of those brightly coloured threads.

It's about people who've had lakes, rivers, streets and schools named after them, statues and monuments erected in their honour, or books and movie scripts written about them. Their stories help us see what life was like and what was going on at key times when Canada was taking shape.

If you read this book all the way through, you'll come away with a sense of how Canada was born. But even if you only read about a few people, I hope you'll take the time to "see" the pages about other people that I point you to. If you do, you'll realize how their stories fit together. If you're just reading about one person, you may come across a phrase or term—such as "seigneurial system," "responsible government" or "Act of Union"—that you wish I'd explained more. If that happens, check out the index. Usually you'll find that it has been explained in a lot more detail in someone else's story.

If history had recorded details of the lives of specific people who lived in Canada thousands of years ago, I would have started the book with some of their stories. And if space had permitted, I would have included many more people. The ones I have chosen represent the thousands of others who helped shape Canada from the time the earliest European explorers arrived up to a point where it begins to look a lot like the country you live in today.

The Penguin Book of
# Canadian Biography
## for Young Readers
# Early Canada

# John Cabot
## (Giovanni Caboto)
### 1449/1450?–1498

JOHN CABOT was probably born in Genoa, Italy, but by the time he was a teenager, he was living in Venice. At that time, Venice was a very busy place. Traders who had made the long trek from Asia filled its canals and harbour, eager to sell their silks, jewels, gold and spices. European merchants crowded around, looking for the best bargains. Often they talked about how much easier it would be if only there were a sea route to China.

Growing up in Venice, Cabot would have heard such talk. He would also have heard of the adventures of Venice's own Marco Polo, who had returned from the Far East two hundred years earlier with tales of the great cities he had visited and the wealth and wonders he had seen.

By the time Cabot was married and the father of three sons, he himself was a merchant. He had also become an expert sailor and a map-maker. As such, he would have known about voyages made by Spanish and Portuguese explorers in search of sea routes to the Orient. Some historians say he may even have been present when Columbus returned to Spain in March 1493, claiming that he had reached the Far East by sailing west.

At the end of the fifteenth century, people still had no idea how big the earth was, so they didn't know that Columbus had only sailed about one-fifth of the way around it. That included Cabot. But he did think that Columbus hadn't sailed far enough to reach Asia. He believed that he could, and that he might be able to find the riches of Cathay that Columbus had missed. As a mariner, he was ready to face the stormy challenges of the Atlantic Ocean. And as a merchant, he was eager to find a way to bypass the middlemen and buy goods directly from Asian suppliers. But making such a voyage would be expensive.

It's not clear how long Cabot spent looking for support for his plans. What is known is that by 1495 he was living in England, home to some of Europe's most experienced sailors. They often sailed the North Atlantic aboard ships searching for new fishing grounds. Rich merchants from the English port city of Bristol outfitted many of those ships. Cabot talked to some of them about his ideas, inviting them to invest in his sea quest. When they agreed, Cabot felt the time had come to ask the most powerful person in England for his support too.

England's king, Henry VII, had heard about what Cabot wanted to do. Not one to pass up a chance to get new lands and wealth for his kingdom, he agreed to listen to details of the plan. Cabot showed the king a map, explaining that he wanted to follow a shorter, more northern route across the Atlantic than Columbus had taken. Once he reached land, he would work his way south along the coast until he found places similar to those described by Marco Polo. That made sense to the king. But when it came to putting up money to help pay for the trip, King Henry decided he wasn't interested. Cabot and his merchant partners would have to be their own bankers.

However, the king did give Cabot and his sons royal permission, or a patent, to take five ships to sail north, west and east, claiming any new lands they found for England. Because of this patent, anyone else who wanted to trade in these new lands would have to ask Cabot first.

King Henry granted Cabot his official permission on March 5, 1496. A few months later, Cabot set sail from Bristol, but his first attempt to cross the Atlantic failed. In the face of stormy weather, food shortages and complaints from his crew, Cabot had to turn back. By the next spring, however, he was ready to try again. On May 2, 1497, he set out in a small, sturdy ship called the *Matthew*. This time, after nearly two months at sea, he sighted land. On June 24, 1497, the adventurous Italian from Venice went ashore and claimed the territory for Henry VII and England.

Historians still aren't sure where Cabot landed. Several think he reached what's now called Cape Breton Island. Others figure that he explored the Newfoundland coast. When he returned to England and reported that he had reached China, he was treated like a hero. People chased him in the streets, eager to hear about his discovery. Merchants were very interested in his descriptions of a sea teeming with millions of codfish, and so was the king. Henry was also pleased to learn that Cabot wanted another chance to find those valuable spices and jewels.

On February 3, 1498, the king gave Cabot permission to take six ships, plus any Englishmen willing to go with him, back to the lands he had found to explore them further and perhaps establish some sort of trading settlement. With the letters patent in hand, Cabot quickly finalized plans with his partners and got ready to sail. In May 1498, he proudly led his small fleet out of Bristol, never to return.

Historians have concluded that Cabot fell victim to the stormy ocean he had so eagerly crossed. But his adventurous spirit would live on in his son Sebastian, who would also become an explorer and a map-maker. And John Cabot's voyage and maps would make it clear to Europeans who came after him that when they followed his route across the Atlantic, they would find not Asia, but an entirely separate continent, North America.

# Jacques Cartier
## 1491–1557

F OR JACQUES CARTIER, born and raised in St-Malo, on the English Channel coast of France, the lure of the sea was irresistible. Powerful tides, salty breezes and the creaking and groaning of ships setting sail were part of the fabric of daily life, and sea captains and pirates were local heroes. By the time he married Catherine Des Granches in 1519, Cartier was well on his way to joining the ranks of those heroes.

In the 1520s, Cartier's reputation as a master mariner and navigator grew as he sailed farther and farther from home. Some historians think he sailed all the way to Brazil and as far as the Strait of Belle Isle, west of Newfoundland. The bishop of St-Malo was so proud of Cartier that he bragged about him to Francis I, the king of France.

At that time, monarchs of other countries, such as Spain, Portugal and England, were sending explorers to the west. In 1534, King Francis decided to send the highly recommended Cartier exploring for him. He ordered Cartier to sail to what Europeans were calling the New World to look for lands rich in gold and other valuable minerals. Cartier was also supposed to keep an eye out for a western route to China.

On May 20, 1534, Cartier led two ships out of St-Malo's harbour. The course he had plotted for the sixty-one men aboard took them directly to the east coast of Newfoundland. He made the trip in twenty days. After a few days at anchor around Cape Bonavista to repair his ships, he was on the move again, sailing north and across the Strait of Belle Isle to the Labrador coast.

Cartier didn't like the barren, rocky land there, complaining that he didn't even see enough soil to fill a cart. So he turned south, moving along Newfoundland's west coast until he reached Cape Breton. Then he steered west, and on June 29 found a much greener, more fertile place that he did like, Prince Edward Island. But Cartier kept going, sailing all the way across the Gulf of St. Lawrence and into a large bay he hoped might be the entrance to a water route to Asia. He arrived there on July 8, a summer's day so hot that he named the place Chaleur Bay. (*Chaleur* means heat or warmth in French.)

After exploring and mapping the bay, Cartier moved north to the Gaspé Peninsula. There, on July 24, he went ashore, put up a nine-metre wooden cross and claimed the land for France. But Cartier and his sailors weren't alone during the cross-raising. Some nearby Iroquois were suspicious of this ceremony taking place on land they came to each summer to fish and hunt seals. Their chief, Donnacona, made it clear that he objected. But Cartier organized a feast for the Native people, and, with a promise to bring them back the following summer, convinced

Donnacona to let two of his sons, Domagaya and Taignongny, go to France as interpreters. Cartier sailed on to Anticosti Island, then turned east and headed home the way he had come.

Cartier didn't realize that he had just missed the entrance to a mighty river that would have taken him deep into the interior of the New World. He hadn't found any gold either. But just a few months after he returned, the king approved a second voyage. On May 19, 1535, Cartier again set out from St-Malo, this time with 110 men and three ships.

After fifty long days, many of them stormy, Cartier reached the Labrador coast. In the next few weeks, he worked his way back down to Anticosti Island. With the help of Donnacona's sons, he found his way into the channel between the island and the mainland, and eventually reached the mouth of the St. Lawrence River. Cartier was excited. Was this the sea route to the Far East?

Cartier soon realized that he had entered a powerful freshwater river and was heading to Stadacona, the Native village, or *kanata,* that his Iroquois interpreters had told him about. He reached Stadacona, where Donnacona was chief, by mid-September. Close by, at the future site of Quebec City, he moored his ships and ordered some of his men to prepare for a winter stay. Then, against Donnacona's wishes, he continued upriver in the smallest ship to Hochelaga.

When Cartier arrived there, the Native people welcomed their French visitors and offered them food. Cartier was impressed with the large village and the corn fields around it. He was also impressed with the magnificent view from a nearby mountain that he named Mount Royal. From atop Mount Royal, he could see the Ottawa River spilling into the St. Lawrence, and he wondered if it would take him to China. But it was too late to find out. The autumn nights were growing colder. By mid-October, Cartier was back at the small fort his men had built at Cap-Rouge, near Stadacona.

The next five months were a nightmare. Bitter cold, heavy snowfalls and a shortage of fresh food left most of Cartier's men sick with scurvy, their legs bloated and covered with sores, their teeth rotting and falling out. Twenty-five men died. Even more would have died if Cartier hadn't learned from Domagaya how to make a tea rich in vitamin C from white cedar bark and leaves.

In early May 1536, just as Cartier was about to leave, he tricked Donnacona, his two sons and seven other Iroquois, including four children, into the fort, took them prisoner and forced them aboard his ship. Then he set sail, promising the warriors who tried to stop him that he'd bring the captives back the following spring.

Cartier was back in St-Malo by mid-July, but four more years passed before he returned to the land he now called Canada (from the Iroquois word *kanata*), and by then all ten Iroquois had died. Francis I put off giving Cartier permission for a third voyage because he wasn't sure it would be a good investment. However, in 1540 he put up enough money to outfit five ships with a total crew of 1,500, again naming Cartier commander of the fleet.

In January 1541, Cartier got disappointing news. The king had changed his mind, putting the Sieur de Roberval in charge instead. Still, Cartier went on with his preparations, and was all ready to go in early May. By the third week of May, Roberval still wasn't ready, so Cartier left on his own with three ships, agreeing to meet up with the others in Newfoundland. After six weeks there, Roberval still hadn't shown up, so Cartier set sail for Stadacona without him.

Cartier arrived there on August 23, and told the Iroquois that their chief had died. He lied about the others, saying they were all living like princes back in France. Then he ordered his men to build a bigger, stronger fort a little way up the St. Charles River. After doing a little exploring upriver, he returned to spend the winter at the new settlement, Charlesbourg.

Scurvy again took its toll. As well, several Iroquois, angry about Donnacona's capture and his death in France, killed forty Frenchmen. By the following June, Cartier decided to abandon Charlesbourg and head for home. When he stopped at St. John's, Newfoundland, on the way back, he finally found his missing commander. Roberval wanted Cartier to report to him the next day, but Cartier couldn't be bothered. Annoyed with Roberval, he sailed out of the harbour during the night and set a course for France, eager to show the king the samples of gold and diamonds his men had found near Charlesbourg.

The gold turned out to be iron pyrite, or fool's gold, and the so-called diamonds were just quartz crystals. Still, King Francis didn't seem to be too annoyed with Cartier, and he let him retire in peace to a big house near St-Malo that he had given him a few years earlier.

Cartier lived there with his wife until she died in 1575. He died two years later, on September 1, 1577. But the tales of his adventures would live on in St-Malo for centuries to come, and he would become known as the first European to return home with news of a New World land called Canada.

# Humphrey Gilbert
## 1537–1583

L IKE SO many others in the sixteenth century, Humphrey Gilbert went to sea in search of fame, fortune and adventure. His family, from Devonshire, England, was wealthy and sent him to one of the world's great universities, Oxford. By the time he was twenty-one, he was living with other student lawyers in London, working for King Henry VIII's daughter, Princess Elizabeth, probably as a clerk.

In 1563, Gilbert became very interested in world geography. The more he learned, the more he became convinced that he could be the one to find a northwest sea passage to the Far East. In 1565 he asked Elizabeth I, who had been crowned queen in 1559, for permission to search for this northwest passage. He was willing to use his own money to pay for the trip, but if he found the route, he wanted a trade monopoly, or total control over any merchants sailing through it. He also suggested populating the passage with poor people who might otherwise be hanged for stealing.

Queen Elizabeth turned him down, but she gave him a job as a military officer in Ireland. He returned to England in 1570 and was knighted by the queen. That same year he married a wealthy woman, Anne Archer. They would have six boys and a girl.

In the next few years, Gilbert served as a member of Parliament for a while. Then he led a thousand-man force Queen Elizabeth sent to help the Dutch fight the Spanish. By the mid-1570s, he was pushing new plans for a voyage of exploration to America. In 1578, Elizabeth gave him letters patent, or royal permission, to claim for England and colonize a place he chose that other European countries hadn't yet claimed as theirs. The land would be Gilbert's to keep for himself or to sell to others. If Gilbert's plan succeeded, he and his friends would become very wealthy, powerful landowners.

By November 1578, he had nearly six hundred men and ten ships loaded with guns, cannons and supplies, all ready to leave port. But many of the crew weren't exactly the best-behaved sailors around. Some were prisoners who'd had a date with the hangman, and some were experienced pirates. One pirate simply took off on his own little cruise with three of the ships. The other seven ships finally sailed on November 18, but they made it only as far as Ireland because some were leaking and others didn't have enough supplies. Gilbert himself tried again in mid-February 1579, but he was back in England by the end of April. Only one ship, with Gilbert's half-brother, Walter Raleigh, as captain, made it partway to the West Indies before it, too, had to turn back.

Gilbert's plan had failed miserably, and it had cost him most of his own money and some of his wife's fortune too. But that just made him all the more determined to start a new colony somewhere in America. The next time, he planned to sail directly to Newfoundland, where Europeans had been fishing for a few hundred years, and then make for the northeast coast of the mainland.

By June 1583, Gilbert was ready to go exploring again. He had pored over all the books, charts, pamphlets and maps he could find, and he had spent a lot of money on materials and equipment to study the plants, animals and minerals of his new colony, wherever that might be. Five ships were anchored at Plymouth, waiting to hoist sails. One was the *Golden Hind*. Its former owner, the famed Sir Francis Drake, had sailed it around the world a few years earlier. Another, the *Bark Raleigh,* belonged to its captain,

Gilbert's half-brother, Walter, who by then was gaining quite a reputation as a great sailor. Gilbert's flagship was the *Squirrel,* and the other two were the *Swallow* and the *Delight.*

The five ships left Plymouth June 11 on what was to be a long and stormy Atlantic crossing. Raleigh had to turn back early on, and the other four didn't meet up at St. John's, Newfoundland, until August 3. But when Gilbert tried to enter the narrow harbour, he was blocked by men from three dozen ships already in port. The Portuguese sailors in particular remembered how one of Gilbert's captains had pirated their ships before, and they weren't about to give him a friendly welcome.

However, when Gilbert showed the port's admiral his letters patent from Queen Elizabeth, the man had to let him enter and drop anchor. That day, August 5, 1583, Gilbert went ashore and claimed Newfoundland for England. He said he was in charge and announced some new laws. For example, he banned public church services for Roman Catholics, and he made it illegal for anyone to insult the queen. Any man who did was to have his ears cut off.

But Gilbert wasn't going to stay around just yet to enforce those laws. He still hadn't checked out America for a place to set up a new colony. By then, though, some of his men were getting fed up. Gilbert had a bad temper and could be a hard man to work for at times. To avoid further trouble, he sent the complainers and some sick crew members back home on the *Swallow,* and then set off again, bound for Sable Island. He planned to stop there to add a few wild pigs and cows to the food supply.

Gilbert wasn't far from Sable when he argued with his navigator and forced him to change course. He shouldn't have done that. Early the next morning, the *Delight* ran aground and broke apart. Dozens of sailors drowned, and needed supplies were lost. With only two ships left, more men started worrying about not getting back to England, and on August 31 Gilbert agreed to turn around.

The two ships sailed close by each other. After a week at sea the skies grew dark and the winds grew stronger. By September 9, waves taller than buildings were tossing the ships around like toy boats. During a brief break in the storm, Gilbert appeared on the *Squirrel*'s deck, shouting, "We are as near to heaven by sea as by land." Later that night, the watch on the *Golden Hind* called out grim news. Gilbert's ship was gone.

The *Golden Hind* made it home with news of what had happened, and of how Gilbert had claimed Newfoundland for England. That would bring him fame. But his search for fortune and adventure ended that September night in 1583, when the sea claimed him and his crew.

# Martin Frobisher

## 1539–1594

S IR MARTIN FROBISHER was pleased. The queen herself, Elizabeth I, was waving goodbye to him as he led his small fleet down the Thames River. She liked this adventure-loving sea captain. He had served her well over the years, battling her enemies and flirting with piracy to add to her wealth. Now, in early June 1576, he was the admiral of the three ships heading out to sea in search of a northwest passage to China, and the queen was showing her support.

Nearly eighty years had passed since England had supported a similar attempt by John Cabot (see p. 1), and it had taken Frobisher fifteen years to find backers willing to help pay for this effort. One in particular, the businessman Michael Lok, had finally put up nearly half the money needed. Both he and

Frobisher figured that if the trip was successful, they and their partners would make a fortune buying and selling spices, gold and jewels from the Far East.

Frobisher's many years at sea had earned him a reputation as one of England's finest sailors. As a boy whose grandfather was a knight, he had had a chance to be educated as a nobleman. But young Frobisher didn't want to study. He longed to go to sea. His uncle, Sir John York, finally decided that might not be a bad idea, and arranged for his fourteen-year-old nephew to join a sailing expedition to the west coast of Africa. Many men died on that voyage, but Frobisher returned home knowing he had found his calling. A mariner he would be.

Twenty-three years later, Frobisher was more than ready for what he saw as the adventure of a lifetime. Calm weather slowed him down as he moved up into the North Sea, but the winds picked up as he neared the Shetland Islands, and at last he was able to set a course west across the Atlantic.

Less than a week later, he was off the coast of Greenland, but there the ice-filled sea turned deadly. Huge waves battered Frobisher's ships, and the smallest one sank with four men on board. Frobisher's ship, the *Gabriel,* took on water, and the third ship, the *Michael,* was blown out to sea. The *Michael's* captain was terrified. As soon as he could, he changed course and sailed home, certain that the *Gabriel* had sunk too.

But Frobisher and his ship had survived the storm, and he was not about to quit. By the end of July he had sighted land, and was soon working his way into what he thought was a channel, or strait, between Asia and North America. He named the channel after himself, having no idea that Frobisher Strait was not a strait at all, but a very deep bay on southern Baffin Island that still bears his name.

As Frobisher explored the bay, some Inuit hunters paddled

out to him to trade their furs and meat for some clothes and a few other items that caught their interest. At one point, five of his men returned to shore with the Inuit, but they didn't come back as planned. Frobisher searched for them for several days, but finally had to make preparations to leave without them. Just before he left, he kidnapped an Inuit trader and forced him to return to England with him.

There was a lot of celebrating when Frobisher, very much alive and well, returned to London on October 9. People were also very interested in his unwilling, and by now sick, passenger and the kayak that Frobisher had brought back. Tragically, the Inuit man died soon after arriving in London, but interest in Frobisher's adventure remained high.

However, investors wanted more than exciting stories in return for their backing. Lok had a yellow-flecked rock Frobisher had collected tested by several experts. Most found no evidence of any valuable minerals, but one claimed that he had found traces of gold. That was all the investors needed to hear. They agreed to support a second voyage for the sole purpose of searching for gold.

By mid-July 1577, Frobisher was back in Frobisher Strait, mining an island in the bay. That summer his men loaded one of their three ships with two hundred tons of what they thought was gold ore. And once more, when he was ready to leave, Frobisher turned kidnapper, capturing an Inuit father, mother and child. All three would also get sick and die soon after reaching England.

The ore Frobisher brought back produced little or no gold, but his investors decided to back one last expedition, a major one designed to collect two thousand tons of ore. On this 1578 voyage, Frobisher had fifteen ships under his command, but storms and pack ice took their toll. One ship sank, and the frightened crew of a second disobeyed orders and returned home. Still, the rest of

Frobisher's men worked hard during the short Arctic summer, digging up tons of rock that would later be shown to contain only iron pyrite, or fool's gold.

Another five years would pass before Frobisher's angry backers finally had to admit that they had spent their money mining and shipping boatloads of worthless rocks. But by then, Frobisher was back doing what he did best, sailing the seas for England and the queen who had once waved goodbye to him.

In 1588, Elizabeth I knighted Frobisher for his efforts in helping Sir Francis Drake defeat the powerful Spanish fleet, or Armada. Six years later, during another fight with Spain, Frobisher's luck ran out. He was shot during an attack on a Spanish-held fort in France. Seriously wounded, he was brought back across the English Channel to Plymouth, where he died on November 22, 1594.

Frobisher was the first European to come in contact with the Inuit living on Baffin Island. In 1987, Frobisher Bay, a community with the same name as the bay, proudly reclaimed its Inuit name, Iqaluit. A hunting camp in Frobisher's time, Iqaluit is now the capital of Canada's newest territory, Nunavut.

# Henry Hudson
## 15??–1611?

**H**ISTORICAL RECORDS don't shed any light on the early life of an Englishman named Henry Hudson. In fact, Hudson doesn't make a recorded appearance until about 1607, when he is already middle-aged. Four years later, he's gone again, leaving behind only his name to mark his visits to the New World.

By 1607, Hudson must have been a very good navigator. Otherwise, the major trading companies he was sailing for wouldn't have trusted him with their ships. Even when he failed, they were impressed. In 1608, one English company sent him in search of a sea passage to China across the top of Russia. When he didn't find it, his employers gave up on the idea. If Hudson couldn't sail through those Arctic waters, they figured nobody could.

But in 1609, the owners of a Dutch company, the Dutch East India Trading Company, hired Hudson to try again. He set sail that spring in a ship called the *Half Moon*. But when he entered the ice-filled waters of the Barents Sea, north of Norway, his crew panicked and told him he had to turn back. Hudson did, but he didn't head home. He kept right on sailing, all the way across the Atlantic. If he couldn't find a northeast passage to the wealth of the Far East, he would look for a northwest one.

Hudson didn't find that either, but he did become the first European to navigate the river named after him all the way to what is now Albany, New York. When he returned with news of that discovery, the English government ordered him to stop exploring for foreign countries. But that didn't mean he was out of work. A group of British merchants came up with the money to send him on another voyage, this time to a place much farther north than the New England coast.

On April 17, 1610, Captain Hudson set sail from London in a ship called the *Discovery*. His destination was the southeast shore of what is now called Baffin Island, where earlier explorers had noticed a possible entrance to a northwest passage. During a brief stopover in Iceland, two of Hudson's men got into a terrible fight, and some of the crew thought Hudson blamed the wrong man for starting it. At sea again, the first mate, Robert Juet, got drunk and tried to turn the crew against Hudson. The captain was furious with him, but he managed to get both his temper and the crew under control again.

Still, tensions simmered. When Hudson finally entered the treacherous 640-kilometre strait that would eventually bear his name, many of the men became very nervous. Ice rammed the ship, and tidal surges swept it dangerously close to rocky shallows. At Akpatok Island, at the top of Ungava Bay, Juet got up to his dirty tricks again, trying to talk the crew into forcing Hudson to turn back. But a few men had remained loyal right from the start, and Hudson pleaded with and scolded the rest until they shaped up. Then he went back to concentrating on moving his ship slowly but safely through the dangerous channel, making careful charts as he went along.

Later that summer, Hudson sent some men to check out a small island near the western end of the strait. They came back saying it would be a great place to rest for a few days. It was covered in the first green grass they'd seen in a long time, and there were plenty of wild birds to add to the food supply. But it seems that Hudson was too excited by then. He felt sure that he would soon reach the northern Pacific and China. Now was not the time to stop.

Maybe Hudson should have stopped. Perhaps, if he had, his rested crew would have been more willing to put up with what lay ahead. But Hudson went on, turning south into the vast, open waters of Hudson Bay. By October he had reached the bay that would one day be named for a later explorer, Thomas James. Slowly it dawned on Hudson that he had reached a dead end. The northwest passage did not go on from there, and it was now too cold to leave.

That winter was horrible. Faced with a limited amount of food, bone-chilling cold and sickness, the men got more and more upset. So did Hudson. He made some bad decisions, threatening some men with pay cuts and showing favouritism towards others. By the time the ice began to break up, tensions had reached the boiling point. Juet and a few others sensed that a mutiny, or takeover by the crew, might finally succeed. They began to spread the word that Hudson was hiding food, and they hinted that with fewer mouths to feed, they'd have a better chance of surviving the long voyage home.

The *Discovery* set sail again on June 12, 1611. But at first light on June 24, the leaders of the mutiny made their move. Hudson, his teenaged son, John, and six others were grabbed and lowered over the edge of the ship into a small sailboat. Just before the boat was set adrift, the ship's carpenter, Philip Staffe, stepped forward. Loyal to the end, he followed his captain overboard.

It would be seven years before any of the mutineers were charged with what they had done, and by then there wasn't enough evidence to convict them. Hudson's discoveries—Hudson River, Hudson Strait and Hudson Bay—would play a major role in drawing others farther into the interior of North America than anyone had gone before. But Hudson never got the hero's welcome he must have dreamed of every now and then. He and the eight others probably starved to death. Only his name, like words carved into northern rocks, remains to remind the world he was there.

# Peter Easton
## (15??–16??)

C LOSE BY Harbour Grace, on Newfoundland's Conception Bay, there's a place people call the Pirates' Graveyard. Almost four hundred years ago, an Englishman named Peter Easton buried forty-seven of his men there. They'd been killed during a battle between Easton and some sailors from the Basque region of France who had taken over Easton's fort while he was away at sea.

Did the Basques think that Easton wouldn't come back to his Harbour Grace headquarters? Or did they think they could beat him off if he did? Whatever their reasons, their actions brought them up against one of the greatest pirates ever to sail the seas, and he wasn't about to let them get away with seizing his property. When Easton's ships appeared in the distance, the Basques sailed out to meet him head-on, but they were no match for his skilful manoeuvring and superior weaponry. His cast-iron cannons found their mark, and his men quickly boarded the Basque ships that hadn't sunk. Then he lowered boats filled with his toughest crew members to go ashore and take back what was his.

The forty-seven men Easton lost that day are not the only pirates buried along Newfoundland's rocky coasts. In the early 1600s, the island was an ideal place for these outlaws to rest up, sort their plunder, fix their ships, get more sailors and supplies and, in the case of Easton, build a fancy house overlooking the sea. It was far enough away from Europe to make it too dangerous and expensive for annoyed kings or queens to send ships to capture the outlaws. Many pirates also liked it because they could zip back there with their loot after raids in the West Indies.

No one was really in charge of Newfoundland at the time. Sir Humphrey Gilbert (see p. 10) had claimed it for England in 1583, but Portuguese, French and Basque merchants and fishermen also sailed freely in and out of St. John's harbour and all around the Avalon Peninsula. Catching and salting fish was a very profitable business then, and there was more than enough to go around. Whaling and lumbering also drew some fortune seekers to the "New Founde Land" in the North Atlantic.

Easton operated out of Newfoundland from 1611 to 1614. He hadn't always been a pirate. His birthdate and birthplace are lost to history, but it is known that he came from an upper-class English family with a long tradition of service to king and country. Even his captives commented on his gentlemanly behaviour. He gained a reputation as a brave and successful sea captain while serving Queen Elizabeth I as a privateer. While England was at war with Spain, Queen Elizabeth made good use of many such gentlemen, who used their own ships to capture enemy vessels and claim all the treasure they found on board.

Easton was still a privateer when he first visited Newfoundland in 1602. He sailed there with an English fishing fleet to protect it from foreign privateers. On the way over, he held up a Dutch privateer and rescued a young Irish woman named Sheila O'Connor, the wife of one of his officers, Gilbert Pike. O'Connor and Pike were two of the earliest permanent settlers in Newfoundland, and they had several children after they were reunited. But Queen Elizabeth I died the next year, and when James I became king and ended the war with Spain, Easton and the other English privateers found that their services were no longer needed. So Easton went into business for himself—as a pirate.

Within a few years, Easton had in effect become the admiral of his own little navy. With more than three dozen ships under his command, all of them very well armed, he ruled the seas he sailed. He even had the nerve—and the wherewithal—to patrol part of the English Channel and collect protection money from ships passing through there. It soon became painfully clear to any captains refusing to pay that the person they needed protection from was Easton himself. He, in turn, paid part of what he collected to the Killigrews, a powerful, aristocratic family that owned a long strip of coastline in Cornwall and let pirates stay in its harbours and coves.

In 1610, after many complaints about the extortion and harassment, King James finally decided to send a well-educated young adventurer named Henry Mainwaring to Cornwall to catch Easton. But Easton heard about what Mainwaring was up to, and when Mainwaring showed up, Easton was gone. He had decided it might be smart to move to Newfoundland for a while. Soon after, Mainwaring turned to privateering, and eventually became a pirate himself.

People living or working in Newfoundland weren't exactly sure what to make of Easton. He not only robbed them, but also captured many of them to work on his ships. When his flagship, the *Happy Adventure,* sailed into view, they definitely weren't happy to see it. But he treated his men well, and he dressed, spoke and acted like such a nice gentleman much of the time. In 1612, he strongly urged John Guy, the first governor of the new English colony in Newfoundland, to come aboard for a visit. Then he kept him on the *Happy Adventure* for two weeks, wining and dining him in his elegant living quarters. Finally, he let him go.

Perhaps the two men found that they liked each other. Maybe they made a deal. Whatever the reason, Easton, from then on, appears to have treated the colonists rather gently—for a pirate, that is. He still raided them, but only one settler was ever killed, and that shooting was accidental. Guy still advised people to fight back if they could, but there really wasn't much point. After all, Easton wasn't called the arch-pirate for nothing. Instead, some folks turned to him occasionally for help. One autumn, for example, the English settlers sailed over to Harbour Grace to leave tons of salt and other supplies with Easton for safekeeping during the winter.

In 1612, Easton captured Sir Richard Whitbourne, a trader who often sailed to Newfoundland to do business with whalers, fishing fleets and Native hunters. Easton kept Whitbourne with him for three and a half months, trying to talk him into becoming a pirate too. When Whitbourne rejected the life of an outlaw, Easton asked him if he would speak with the king on his behalf when he returned to England. He wanted Whitbourne to convince the king that he didn't want to be a pirate any more and should be pardoned. When Whitbourne agreed to do this, Easton released him.

What Easton didn't know was that King James had already pardoned him that spring. The official papers saying he wouldn't be punished never reached him, nor did news of a second pardon, given late that year on Whitbourne's advice. In 1614, Easton packed up all the gold he had taken from Spanish and English ships sailing the Caribbean, cleaned out the mansion he had built at Ferryland, south of St. John's, and sailed away with fourteen ships. He stopped at the Azores, islands in the Atlantic, just long enough to ambush the large Spanish fleet that was transporting the year's loot from Central America back to Spain. Then, with four extra Spanish ships under his command, he sailed on to North Africa's Barbary Coast.

Pirates loved the Barbary Coast. They were free to come and go there as they pleased. Easton stayed there for about a year before offering his services to the duke of Savoy, who ruled part of France on the Mediterranean coast. The duke was happy to have such an experienced fighting seaman on his side, so Easton moved to the Riviera. There, with a fortune that would be worth nearly half a billion dollars today, he bought himself a palace, started living like a prince and soon faded from history.

Several of Easton's sailors took his last name when they settled in Newfoundland and started their own families. In fact, the name Easton is still quite common in Canada's easternmost province. There's also a place there called Happy Adventure. It and the Pirates' Graveyard are just two of the island's many links with one of its most famous residents, the arch-pirate Peter Easton.

# Samuel de Champlain
## 1570?–1635

**A**FTER JACQUES CARTIER (see p. 5) returned to France in 1542, interest in exploring Canada faded, especially when the gold and diamonds he brought back turned out to be fool's gold and quartz crystals. Some people even went so far as to make jokes about the place. Anything that sparkled or looked expensive but was really worthless came to be known as a Canadian diamond. But for Samuel de Champlain, Canada was no joking matter. It would become his life's work.

Champlain came from Brouage, a small Atlantic seaport midway down the French coast. Extracting salt from sea water was big business there—it was used to keep fish and meat from going bad, and ships were always sailing into port to load up with it. Champlain's father sailed on some of those ships, and as soon as he was big enough, Champlain himself went to sea. At first, he just went fishing or followed the coastline for a bit in a small rowboat. When he was older, his uncle took him on a voyage to Spain, and there's some evidence that he even took him all the way to the West Indies.

Champlain never tired of going to sea, and he learned everything he could about plotting courses, navigating through unknown waters and making detailed maps and charts. But he had to earn a living too, so in his late teens he became a soldier in the French army, which was then fighting the Spanish. In 1603, he jumped at an invitation to sail to New France with François Gravé Du Pont, a man with whom he would become good friends. He went along on that voyage as a sort of unofficial historian and geographer.

At the end of May, Gravé's ship, the *Bonne-Renommée*, arrived at Tadoussac, which was then France's main fur-trading centre on the St. Lawrence River. Gravé was acting for the company that held a monopoly on, or owned, the trading rights in New France. While Gravé dealt with the traders, Champlain spent time getting to know the Montagnais and Huron he met there. He also did a bit of exploring, canoeing about 60 kilometres up the Saguenay River.

By mid-June, Gravé and Champlain were back on the *Bonne-Renommée*, sailing up the St. Lawrence. As he passed one place—the future site of Quebec—Champlain noted that it might be a good spot for a settlement. Farther along, he stopped to explore about 30 kilometres of the Richelieu River. The Lachine Rapids, near Montreal, finally forced Gravé to turn back, but not before Champlain had learned a lot from the Native guides about five great lakes and a large waterfall that lay beyond. He trusted what they told him, and included their information on his maps when he got back to France.

Champlain now figured that Acadia (now the Maritime provinces) would be a better place for a permanent settlement because it was warmer there than at Tadoussac. The new holder of the trading monopoly, Pierre du Gua, Sieur de Monts, agreed with him, and lined up three ships and nearly one hundred men—a mixture of gentlemen, skilled craftsmen and ex-convicts—to establish the settlement.

De Monts, Champlain and Gravé sailed from France in the spring of 1604. When they reached the east coast of Canada, Champlain spent a few weeks checking out the Acadia region for a good location. He liked one spot in the Bay of Fundy—in fact, de Monts would build Port Royal there in 1605—but he finally chose an island in the St. Croix River, at the southeast tip of what's now New Brunswick. Work on building the village and planting crops began immediately.

In the meantime, Champlain did some more exploring. He sailed up the Bay of Fundy to what is now Saint John, where he met and feasted with some Mi'kmaqs living in the area. He also followed the Nova Scotia and Maine coastline, making detailed maps and harbour charts along the way. When he returned to St. Croix at the beginning of October, he found a cozy nest of new buildings, complete with windows from France, on the island.

That winter, however, was anything but cozy. The buildings had kept out the vicious blackflies, but they couldn't keep out the numbing winter cold. Even the wine froze and had to be carved out in chunks. Ice jams cut the settlers off from their only supply of fresh water on the mainland, and food supplies ran low. Thirty-five men died of scurvy. In the spring, de Monts decided to abandon the settlement and try again at Port Royal.

Champlain stayed at Port Royal from 1605 to 1607, exploring and learning more about what it would take to survive in New France. He now knew how harsh winter could be, how much the

Aboriginal people knew about the country's geography and how valuable their friendship was. He'd also learned how important it was to keep people's spirits up in tough times. During the winter of 1606–7, he set up the Order of Good Cheer. Members of the order took turns acting as host, coming up with great meals and entertainment for their guests, the rest of the French settlers and Mi'kmaqs at Port Royal.

In 1607, de Monts lost his monopoly, so he couldn't afford to keep up the settlement. He abandoned Port Royal, and after a little more exploring, Champlain and he returned to France. But in 1608, Champlain was back, this time at the place on the St. Lawrence he had noticed in 1603. As de Monts's lieutenant, his job was to build a trading post there, closer to the fur trade. He wanted this settlement to last, and it did, eventually growing into Quebec's capital, Quebec City.

The next few years were never dull for Champlain. The first summer he headed off a plot to kill him, and the first winter he watched helplessly as sixteen of the twenty-five settlers died of scurvy. The next year he travelled with a group of Huron, Algonquin and Montagnais all the way up the Richelieu River to the lake named after him. There, he was drawn into a battle between his travelling companions and attacking Iroquois, and he shot two of their chiefs. His gun frightened the Iroquois, but the deaths of their chiefs enraged them. From then on, the French were their sworn enemies. Champlain promised the Huron he'd be on their side.

In 1615, Champlain travelled by canoe up the Ottawa River and all the way to Huronia, on southern Georgian Bay, then home to the villages of nearly ten thousand Huron (the Wendat nation). Then, to keep his promise, he joined several hundred Native warriors who paddled and portaged down to and across Lake Ontario to attack the Iroquois. Champlain was wounded in the knee during the battle and had to be carried away when the Huron abandoned their war canoes and retreated on foot. Champlain had to spend the winter with them at Huronia.

Champlain also went back to France many times. On one trip home, in 1610, he decided to get married. He arranged with the Boullé family to marry their daughter, Hélène, who was only twelve at the time. The couple was married at Christmas, but Hélène stayed with her parents for nearly three years before moving to Champlain's house in Paris. She didn't sail with Champlain to Quebec until 1620. But the Habitation, Champlain's name for the fortified buildings, was in pretty rough shape, and she was very unhappy and lonely there. Four years later she moved back to France, where she managed her husband's affairs while he was away. She and Champlain never had any children.

Whenever Champlain was in France, he did everything he could for the Quebec settlement. He tried to talk skilled tradesmen and farmers into going there, but without much success. Some Catholic missionary priests wanted to go. They were eager to try to convert the Native peoples to Christianity. But funding for the colony depended on who held political power at the time and who controlled the fur trade. French merchants and investors were getting rich, but they weren't willing to spend their profits on sending supplies and settlers to New France. By 1626, there were still only fifty or so people in the colony, and life was difficult.

In 1627, war broke out between France and England, and the next year a fleet led by five English brothers, the Kirkes, tried to take Canada from the French. They cut off supply ships downriver, but Champlain pretended that everything was fine, and that the Habitation could defend itself. The Kirkes decided to wait until the following spring to show up at Quebec. By then, there was hardly any food left in the fort, and Champlain had no choice but to surrender. The Kirkes took him back to England, but a few months later he was allowed to return to France.

In 1632, a peace treaty was worked out that gave Quebec back to the French, and in 1633 Champlain was put in charge of New France for the first time. But he wasn't named governor, an honour that should have been his. Still, all Champlain cared about was his beloved settlement. By then in his early sixties, he sailed back and worked as hard as ever, taking care of the colony's business. He even started building two new habitations, one near Quebec and one at Trois-Rivières. But in 1635, his health began to fail. That October he had a terrible stroke that left him paralyzed, and two months later, on Christmas Day, he was dead. For many settlers, it was as if their father had died.

There were still only about 150 people in the colony that Christmas, but the foundations laid down by Champlain were strong and lasting. They were the foundations on which a great new country would be built.

# Étienne Brûlé

## 1592?–1633

É TIENNE BRÛLÉ was just a teenager when he came to New France with Samuel de Champlain (see p. 27), probably on his third voyage over, in 1608. It's fairly certain he was the young servant Champlain mentioned in his writings about that trip. He was definitely one of twenty-five men who stayed with Champlain during the first bitterly cold winter at Quebec. Sixteen of them died of scurvy, but young Brûlé remained strong and fit. He spent much of the winter with some Montagnais people camped outside the fortified habitation, and he learned a lot about their customs and traditions. He also learned how to speak their language, something Champlain never seemed to be able to do.

In the spring of 1610, Champlain led some Huron allies

against their Iroquois foes just east of Montreal on the south shore of the St. Lawrence. The day after the Iroquois were forced to retreat, Brûlé told Champlain that he wanted to stay with the Huron for a while. Champlain liked the idea. He figured this was a good opportunity for the young man to learn another language and become an interpreter. He also hoped Brûlé would gain valuable information about the water routes the Natives followed, the existence of any mines and mineral deposits, and the locations of other First Nations people. Besides, Brûlé loved adventure and seemed to prefer the Native lifestyle to that of his countrymen.

Champlain agreed to let Brûlé stay with an Algonquin chief, Iroquet, who lived in Huron territory. Iroquet promised to take care of him, and Champlain made a similar promise about a young warrior known as Savignon, whom the Huron insisted Champlain take back to France for a visit. Plans were made to return the two young men to their own people the following June.

The reunion took place June 13, 1611, just west of Montreal. Champlain was waiting for Brûlé near the almost impassable Saint-Louis rapids. Later, he would report that Brûlé had shot those rapids alone, an amazing feat for a young European, and one that proved how skilful a canoeist Brûlé had become. Brûlé had changed in other ways too. He was wearing Native clothing and could speak fluently with his Huron and Algonquin companions. He had also travelled where no European had gone before, up the Ottawa River and over to Georgian Bay.

Brûlé stayed with Champlain just long enough to tell him about all he had seen and learned. Then he was off again, apparently living in Huron territory for the next four years. His next appearance in historical records was in 1615. That summer he was part of another French–Huron expedition against the Iroquois, or Five Nations, Confederacy. Champlain and a large party of

Hurons gathered at Lake Simcoe late in August to make final preparations for their move south into Iroquois territory. There, Brûlé asked to join twelve Huron warriors being sent ahead to warn the friendly Susquehannah of the planned attack and to ask them for reinforcements.

To reach the Susquehannah, Brûlé's small party had to work its way down Lake Simcoe, along the Humber River to Lake Ontario, and across it into what is now upstate New York. Then came the most dangerous part of the journey. The Seneca were part of the Iroquois Confederacy, and the Huron had to sneak through their territory to get to their Susquehannah allies. All went well until some Seneca hunters spotted them. The Seneca attacked, but Brûlé and the Huron fought them off, killing four of them and capturing another two.

Prisoners were like battle trophies for Native warriors. They could be exchanged for other captives, they could be adopted or they could be tortured and burned at the stake at a victory feast. Unfortunately for the two Seneca, they met the last fate when Brûlé and the Huron delivered them to the Susquehannah. But the celebrations went on for several days, putting Brûlé's party way behind schedule. When he and the reinforcements finally made it to Lake Onondaga, where the Champlain-led attack was to take place, they were too late. The battle was already over, and the Huron had lost. A wounded Champlain had to be carried back to Georgian Bay, but Brûlé didn't go with him. He decided to stay with the Susquehannah and explore new territory.

Brûlé didn't write about his travels, but Champlain would later record what he told him about his adventures south of Lake Ontario. It looks as if Brûlé was the first European to travel overland all the way to Chesapeake Bay, on the Atlantic coast. He was also most likely the first European to reach what is now Pennsylvania. According to Champlain's journals, he had a terrifying brush with death, too, when he was captured by some Seneca warriors.

Brûlé reported that he was tortured and tied to a stake to be burned, but that at the last second, he managed to escape the flames. He claimed that just as a Seneca was about to snatch a religious medal from around his neck, he told him that his Christian god would destroy the Seneca. At that moment, thunder exploded from storm clouds overhead, convincing the Seneca that they had better let him go. Brûlé may have made up the part about the religious medal and the miraculous thunder. He was no longer a practising Christian, and had adopted many of the Natives' spiritual rituals as his own. But Champlain believed him, and his missing fingernails were certainly proof that the Seneca hadn't been very friendly towards him.

Between 1621 and 1623, Brûlé did a lot of exploring for Champlain, who was still hoping to find a northwest passage to the Far East. He found the copper deposits the Huron mined on the north shore of Georgian Bay, made it all the way west to Lake Superior and probably journeyed all the way down to Lake Erie too. Over the years, Brûlé also made a lot of valuable contacts with Native hunters interested in trading their furs for European knives, pots, tools, beads and weapons. For an annual fee about ten times that of a labourer's yearly wage, he sent a lot of fur-trade business to the Company of One Hundred Associates, which controlled the fur trade in New France.

Brûlé helped the Jesuit missionaries too, acting as their guide and interpreter when they moved into his home territory in Huron country. The Huron didn't much like the Jesuits at first, and if their friend Brûlé hadn't brought them, they might not have been allowed to stay. But the Jesuits weren't thrilled about needing Brûlé's help. In fact, they didn't like him at all. His lifestyle went completely against the moral standards they were trying to convince the Huron to adopt. Although they said that men should have only one wife, and that couples should get married, Brûlé moved from one Native girlfriend to another, often getting them pregnant. He also got drunk, cursed and swore, broke the rule against eating meat on Fridays, didn't go to Mass or say his prayers, and took part in what the priests saw as some horrifying pagan customs.

But Brûlé wasn't the only Frenchman who had gone to live in the wilderness. These men, who became known as *coureurs de bois* (runners of the woods), were a rough, tough lot, but they needed to be to survive. They made a living illegally buying and selling furs, instead of bringing them all back to Company of One Hundred Associates officials. But at the same time, they explored a lot of new territory for the French and attracted Native traders to Quebec and Tadoussac. They were also worth their weight in gold as interpreters and guides, and as middlemen between the French and the Aboriginals.

So if it hadn't been for his betrayal of Champlain, Brûlé might have gone down in history as a great, courageous explorer and adventurer. But in 1628, when England and France were at war, five brothers named Kirke sailed into the Gulf of the St. Lawrence to take control of New France for the British. When Champlain heard rumours that they were on the way to Quebec, he sent Brûlé downriver to scout out the situation. The Kirkes made it to Quebec and kept the colony under siege all winter. Without supplies from France, the settlers barely survived the winter, and in the spring Champlain had to surrender. When he was taken to one of the Kirkes' ships, he was horrified and enraged to find Brûlé on board. The young servant he had brought with him twenty years earlier had joined the Kirkes and had actually helped them navigate the river.

A few people stayed on in New France when the Kirkes left

with their French prisoners. Brûlé, now branded a traitor, was one of those. He went back to live with the Huron. He died in 1633, the same year Champlain returned to Quebec after a peace settlement between England and France. Maybe he got in a fight with some Huron warriors, or perhaps they just got fed up with him. Whatever the reason, Brûlé died as the two Seneca prisoners had years before. The story of his death includes gory details about his body being eaten afterwards, but a few historians aren't convinced that happened, especially since there was a big argument later about reburying his body and having the Jesuits bless his remains.

When the French returned to Canada, all the Huron were afraid they would pay dearly for Brûlé's death. The villagers where he had been killed were already suffering because of it. They abandoned their village of Toanché, near Penetanguishene, and were hit with a series of illnesses that they blamed on the avenging spirits of Brûlé's relatives. But Champlain wasn't sorry to be rid of Brûlé, and he did nothing to get back at his killers. In fact, if he'd had his way, he probably would have erased his name from history.

# Paul de Chomedey
# de Maisonneuve
## (1612–1676)

P AUL DE CHOMEDEY DE MAISONNEUVE was born into a noble family in the province of Champagne, France. He had been a soldier since he was a young teenager, and for nearly fifteen years had served his country bravely and well. He had also earned a reputation as a good and honest man who was still guided by the spiritual values passed on to him by his family. So when a group of people hoping to start a missionary colony in New France began looking for a leader with military experience, his name came up.

The Society of Montreal (Les Messieurs et Dames de la Societé de Nôtre Dame de Montréal) was the group that wanted Maisonneuve. It was formed after a tax collector, Jérôme le Royer de La Dauversière, told some friends that he had had a vision. In this vision he saw an island near where two great rivers met, and he felt sure that God was calling him to establish a mission there. According to La Dauversière, the island of his vision was Montreal, where the Ottawa River surged into the St. Lawrence.

La Dauversière was a man of strong religious faith who spent both time and money helping people in need. So when he spoke of his vision, he inspired other pious people to believe in it too. In the late 1630s, he and a small group of followers formed the Society of Montreal to raise enough money to buy the island from the seigneur who'd been granted it. They also raised funds to send volunteers there to work with Native people and convert them to Christianity.

Father Charles Lalemant, the first head of the Jesuits in Quebec, was living back in France when he heard of the society's plans. He knew better than most what challenges the volunteers would face in Canada, and how important a strong leader would be in the first years of struggle. It was he who told La Dauversière about Maisonneuve and suggested he meet with him. La Dauversière did, and was very impressed with the man. He asked him to be the governor of the new colony.

By then, Maisonneuve had retired from the army. He was still single, and his financial affairs were in good order, so he was free to accept La Dauversière's offer. But he had a better sense than La Dauversière of just how isolated the little settlement would be, and he knew that it would most likely be attacked by warring Iroquois resisting French moves into their territory. Still, he admired the volunteers who were already willing to go, and he realized that someone with his military experience would be able to help them protect themselves. After praying for guidance, he decided that joining them would be a way that he, too, could live his religious faith more fully.

Once he agreed to be governor, Maisonneuve became very involved in preparations for the group's voyage. He contributed some of his own money to the cause and urged others to make donations. He also recruited a woman named Jeanne Mance (see p. 45) to be the colony's first nurse. Then he helped organize the supplies that would be needed and made arrangements for the group's passage on two ships.

Both ships sailed from France on May 9, 1641, but the one with Maisonneuve on board had a terrible, stormy crossing and didn't reach Quebec until September. New France's governor, Charles Huault de Montmagny, was there to greet him, together with Jeanne Mance and some of the society's other volunteers who had arrived on the first ship a month earlier. However, Maisonneuve soon realized that even though Montmagny and other residents had given the newcomers a warm welcome, they weren't happy with the idea of starting a new colony at Montreal.

New France still had only about two hundred settlers, most of them living at Quebec and Trois-Rivières. It was already hard enough defending these two areas and keeping them supplied with food, clothes and equipment from France. Having to worry about far-off Montreal would just cause more problems. Besides, some business-minded people who were hoping to take control of the fur trade when peace was made with the Mohawk nation figured that a settlement at Montreal might siphon off some of that trade from Quebec.

Nevertheless, Maisonneuve felt duty bound to do what the Society of Montreal wanted, and in the end Montmagny had to go along with him. After a few weeks' rest, Maisonneuve sailed up the St. Lawrence to check out the best site on the island for his nearly five dozen settlers to begin their new life. Then he returned to Quebec and spent the winter giving the group moral support and supervising the building of the boats they would need to take their supplies to Montreal. In the spring, they were ready to go, and on May 17, 1642, they finally arrived at what would be their new home.

Governor Montmagny travelled with Maisonneuve and officially turned the island over to him on May 17. After a religious service led by Father Vimont, then the Jesuit missionaries' leader in Canada, it was time to start work. Bark tents had to be put up, and the sooner a protective palisade, or pointed log wall, was begun, the better. As was so often the case, Maisonneuve led by example. Even though he was the governor, he insisted on cutting down the first tree himself, and he pitched in wherever he was needed. Many hours later, some very tired people, Maisonneuve included, slipped into their tents as darkness fell on Ville-Marie, the name the settlers had given the place in honour of Jesus' mother, Mary.

The first year at Montreal was exhausting but peaceful. Maisonneuve organized the building of the fort and a large habitation that included a chapel and could house six dozen people. The St. Lawrence flooded its banks near the end of December, and rising water threatened the building for a few days, but no one got sick that winter and spirits remained high. It would be another few months before the first war cries of Mohawk fighters pierced the air.

Perhaps the Iroquois hadn't discovered that the French were on the island until late spring. Or maybe they had just been waiting and watching to see if the newcomers were planning to stay. Whatever the explanation, life at Montreal changed dramatically once the sneak attacks started. People had to be very careful when they went fishing or worked in the gardens, and they spent much of their time inside the palisade walls. In June, six men were captured while chopping wood. Only one managed to escape, but not before he had been tortured for hours.

Many of the men became frustrated and urged Maisonneuve to fight back. But he realized that the French were no match for the Native warriors when it came to guerrilla-type warfare, and he thought such a move would be foolish. Unfortunately, he was proved right when he finally agreed to an attack at the end of March 1644. That time, Maisonneuve bravely led thirty settlers into the woods to take on two hundred Iroquois hiding there. With ammunition running low, Maisonneuve finally ordered a retreat, making sure the wounded were safe behind him. But when his men caught sight of the fort, they broke ranks and made a run for it, leaving Maisonneuve alone to hold back his pursuers. He barely escaped with his life.

Maisonneuve also fought for the residents of Ville-Marie in many other ways. He won support for the colony from King Louis XIII, who donated a ship and guaranteed that he would send it across with supplies every year. He worked hard to ensure the success of Jeanne Mance's hospital and Marguerite Bourgeoys's school, both of which served Native and French people alike. When years of Iroquois attacks threatened the colony's very existence, he organized the men into a well-trained militia and headed back to France to talk more soldiers and settlers into returning to Montreal with him. He also spent a lot of time trying to convince different Quebec governors that Montreal deserved their support.

Maisonneuve's own high moral standards served as an example for people living at Ville-Marie too. He personally assigned land grants to those willing to clear and farm a section, but unlike many other officials, he never claimed any land for himself. He managed the settlement's financial affairs carefully and honestly, and did what he could to stop the trading of alcohol to Natives. When Louis XIV came to the throne and reorganized the colony's government and fur trade in the early 1660s, Maisonneuve tried to keep Montreal from becoming a wild, unruly outpost for *coureurs de bois* who didn't want to follow the new fur-trading rules.

But times were changing quickly in New France. In 1665, the king sent out the marquis de Tracy, Alexandre de Prouville, with hundreds of new soldiers to fight the Iroquois. A lasting peace finally looked like a possibility, and merchant traders eagerly awaited the chance to make fortunes from the ever-expanding fur trade. Apparently, Tracy didn't think Montreal's governor fit into this new political scene. In September 1665, he ordered

Maisonneuve to return to France for an indefinite stay. Always one to obey the call of duty, Maisonneuve arranged to sail from Quebec on the next ship out.

The people of Ville-Marie were very sad when they learned that Maisonneuve was leaving them. He had served them bravely, humbly and faithfully for twenty-four years. He returned later that fall to Paris, where he lived simply and quietly until his death in 1676. His one self-indulgence was a small wooden cabin he had built in his garden. Every now and then, he would slip out to that little cabin. Inside, the man who would become known as the founder of Montreal would recall the time he spent on a faraway island, near where two mighty rivers met. The cabin reminded him of home.

# Jeanne Mance
## 1606–1673

EANNE MANCE'S first day on the island of Montreal was coming to an end. Earlier that day she and the rest of the four dozen or so settlers led by Paul de Chomedey de Maisonneuve (see p. 39) had gathered around a makeshift wooden altar to pray for the success of their new colony. After the service, everyone had pitched in to cut wood, put up birchbark tents and unpack a few supplies. Now night was closing in on them, and they had no candles or lamps. Mance and the three other women in the group pocketed some small glass medicine bottles and slipped away from the tents. When they returned, the bottles were glowing. That night, May 17, 1642, Mance and the other settlers drifted off to sleep comforted by the soft flickering light of fireflies.

A year earlier, Mance had been in Paris, France, preparing for bed each evening in a room lit with fine candelabra. But she hadn't gone to Paris to live the good life. She had gone there to learn more about New France, and to figure out how she could best be of service there. A few people wondered why a single woman who wasn't a nun would want to go there, but that didn't bother Mance. People had wondered about some of her life choices before.

Baptized November 12, 1606 (her actual birthdate is unknown), Mance grew up in a large, well-to-do family living in Langres, in the French district of Champagne. As a very attractive young woman, she had caught the eye of many eligible men, but she refused to get engaged to any of them. When she was about twenty years old, her mother died. Marriage then would have given her a certain amount of independence from her large family of five sisters and six brothers, ten of them younger than she was. But she chose to stay at home and help her father care for them and manage the household.

Mance's father died about ten years later, and by 1640 her brothers and sisters were old enough to take care of themselves. Mance was now free to do what she wanted. She had already spent many years caring for others, including the sick and the poor living in her parish, and she felt called to keep doing that kind of work. When a cousin told her about his brother, a young Jesuit priest who had just gone to Canada as a missionary, she was eager to learn more about life there.

Mance began to think about going to New France too. Perhaps she could help the settlers and Native people in some way. She prayed for guidance and turned to a local priest for advice. He gave her the names of some people in Paris to talk to, and as soon as she could make arrangements, she headed to the city to meet with them. A very wealthy widow who wanted to remain anonymous was so impressed with Mance that she offered to give her money to set up a hospital in a new settlement on an island in the St. Lawrence River hundreds of kilometres south of Quebec.

That's how, one year later, Mance ended up on one of two ships sailing to New France with the would-be founders of Montreal on board. Her ship left the French port of La Rochelle on May 9, 1641. The second ship carried Maisonneuve, who'd been named governor of the new colony. The group spent the winter at Quebec, but as soon as the ice left the river in the spring, they were on their way up the St. Lawrence. May 17, 1642, their first day on the island, is given as the founding date of Montreal, or Ville-Marie.

The summer flew by in a flurry of chopping, sawing, building and planting, and a palisade, or log wall, was put up to defend the main buildings against attacks by the Iroquois, who were at war with New France at the time. Mance began caring for the sick that fall. In March 1644, she had to draw on all her nursing skills and stamina when several of Maisonneuve's men were seriously wounded during a fight with a large band of Native warriors in the woods near the fort.

Mance's hospital wasn't finished until 1645. It had to be built on land outside the crowded little fort. Once, when Mance was alone there, Iroquois warriors tried to get in, but some men rushed over from the fort and drove them off. Around 1650, when the conflict between the French and the Iroquois heightened, Mance had to move her beds and medicines back inside the palisades so the hospital building could be used as an extra defence post. During that period, she shared space with a woman named Marguerite Bourgeoys (see p. 49), who had started the colony's first school. Mance cared for patients in the two rooms downstairs, and Bourgeoys taught her students in the small attic above.

In 1649, Mance went to France for a year to get more money for her hospital. Once again, people were impressed by this dedicated, soft-spoken woman, and they gave her their support. Nine years later, she travelled to France again, but this time her health was not good, and she was in a lot of pain. The winter before, she'd had a nasty fall on some ice. Her arm was badly broken and her wrist was dislocated. The fractures healed, but she lost the use of her arm. When she reached La Rochelle, she had to be carried to her destination on a stretcher.

But pain and sickness didn't stop Mance from doing what she had come to do. She got more money for her cause and arranged to have three nursing sisters return to Montreal with her to help run the hospital. She also got something no money could buy: she regained the use of her arm. Mance saw that as a blessing from God. The pain had disappeared right after she touched her arm with a holy object, or relic.

Mance's last years were not as pleasant and comfortable as they should have been. A new company took over the Montreal colony in 1662, and in 1665 Maisonneuve was ordered back to France. The new people in charge weren't as supportive of Mance's work as he had been. But with the help of the nuns, Mance kept running the hospital until she was too weak to do so, in 1673. On June 18 that year, the Angel of Ville-Marie, as she had come to be known, died—and the entire colony mourned her passing.

# Marguerite Bourgeoys
## 1620–1700

MARGUERITE BOURGEOYS was born on April 17, 1620, at Troyes, France, in the province of Champagne. Her father, a candle merchant and coin maker, earned more than enough to take care of his large family, and Bourgeoys had a happy, easy childhood. She enjoyed going to school, and often played school at home with her younger brothers and sisters. As a teenager, she liked wearing pretty clothes and spending time chatting with her girlfriends, but she did her share of housework too. With twelve children to care for, her mother appreciated all the help she could get.

When Bourgeoys was nineteen, and the youngest child was still just a toddler, her mother died. From then on, she and her older sister Anne spent a lot more time helping out at home. But when she was twenty, Bourgeoys also began spending time at a nearby convent. The Catholic nuns there were cloistered. That meant that they couldn't leave the convent to work in the town. However, young women were allowed to go there for religious instruction classes. Bourgeoys started doing that.

Over the next few years, she became convinced that God was calling her to live a more spiritual existence. She thought about becoming a nun, but she didn't want a cloistered life. She wanted to work with and help people where they lived. Sometimes, she and Sister Louise, the convent's Mother Superior, would talk about New France. Sister Louise's brother, Paul de Chomedey de Maisonneuve (see p. 39), lived there. He had founded a small settlement called Ville-Marie on the island of Montreal, and he was also governor of the island. Bourgeoys was fascinated by what Sister Louise told her, and often dreamed about working there.

Once, when Maisonneuve was back in France on business, he went to Troyes to visit his sister. He asked her if she thought one of the women who met regularly at the convent would be willing to go to Ville-Marie. He wanted a layperson—one who hadn't taken religious vows—because she wouldn't have to be cloistered the way all missionary sisters had to be at that time. Sister Louise knew just the person to ask. She introduced her brother to Bourgeoys.

Maisonneuve didn't sugar-coat what life would be like for Bourgeoys at Montreal. He explained that there were still no schoolchildren in the colony. Of the few babies born there so far, most had died. He also told her about the bitterly cold winters, the supply shortages and the surprise attacks by Iroquois warriors. But as Bourgeoys listened, she felt sure that teaching French and Native children in New France was what God wanted her to do. She told Maisonneuve that she would go.

Bourgeoys sailed from France with Maisonneuve on July 20, 1653. After just a few days, people started coming down with high fevers and chills. Bourgeoys worked tirelessly nursing the sick. Eight men died on the voyage. With no priest on board, crew members and passengers alike gathered around Bourgeoys on deck to lead them in prayers for the burials at sea. Her good work had already begun.

The disease-ridden ship landed at Quebec in late September. Jeanne Mance (see p. 45), Montreal's first nurse, was there to greet the governor, and he introduced the two women who would spend the rest of their lives helping the people of Ville-Marie. After several delays, they and the hundred extra men Maisonneuve had brought over to reinforce his small settlement finally reached Montreal on November 16. With the new arrivals, the island colony now had a population of just under two hundred.

It didn't take long for people to see what a hard-working and generous person Bourgeoys was. When she first arrived, she stayed at Maisonneuve's house and helped him run his household. Within days, though, she was also visiting sick settlers, praying with and comforting the dying, washing clothes for the soldiers and doing extra sewing in exchange for things she needed.

But four years passed before there were enough children and any free space at Ville-Marie for Bourgeoys to open her long-awaited school. In 1658, Maisonneuve gave her a small stone stable. She had the place cleaned up and set up sleeping quarters in the tiny attic. The classroom was to be on the ground floor. Finally, on April 30, 1658, Bourgeoys welcomed her first students, five boys and three girls.

From the beginning, Bourgeoys made it clear that she would teach all youngsters, not just those who came from wealthier families. She would teach for free and would live very simply, like the poor people she wanted to help. She also welcomed Native students. She herself became the foster mother to a little Iroquois girl, and she adopted two others. Sadly, all three died before they were old enough to attend her school.

Over time Bourgeoys was able to convince three other women to work with her at Ville-Marie. She also managed to persuade the governor and several settlers to give her another building and some more land for her school. She and the other teachers lived together as if they were in a convent, and people called them sisters, but they didn't take religious vows. Not that Bourgeoys was against their doing that. She actually wished she could start a religious order at Montreal. But church officials would have insisted that the women be cloistered for their own protection, and that was the last thing Bourgeoys wanted. There was too much work that cloistered sisters would never be allowed to do.

In the early 1660s, Bourgeoys opened her home to some *filles du roi,* young single women King Louis XIV was sending to France as would-be wives for the men settling there. She gave them room and board, and taught them basic housekeeping skills that would prepare them for married life in New France. She also checked out the men who wanted to marry them to make sure they would be good husbands.

In 1665, Bourgeoys opened what in effect was Canada's first household-sciences school for older girls. She wanted to make sure all young women had the skills they would need to take care of themselves and their families in an isolated settlement. Her teenaged pupils learned such things as spinning, weaving, dress-making and knitting.

It's also fair to say that Bourgeoys served as New France's first social worker. When former students had problems, they came to her for advice. She helped parents take care of their children and supported couples having trouble in their marriages. She also gave religious education classes to prepare children to make their First Communion.

In 1669, Bourgeoys expanded her school again, adding a new building nearly 30 metres long. But she still had only three other teachers. By then, New France's Governor Daniel de Rémy de Courcelle, Bishop François de Laval and Intendant Jean Talon were all so impressed with her work that they were encouraging her to send teachers to other parts of the colony. She definitely needed more teachers. As well, the governor had told her that it was time she got official approval from the king, or letters patent, for her operations.

In 1670, Bourgeoys sailed to France to do that, but when she got there she found that the king wasn't in Paris. He was off in Dunkirk, on the north coast, preparing for war against Holland. After months of waiting, Bourgeoys decided to go to him. Armed with a letter of introduction from one of Louis's powerful advisers, she showed up at the camp of more than a hundred thousand soldiers and convinced officials to take her to the king's tent. Nervous but determined, she told the king about her work. He too was impressed, especially when he learned that Bourgeoys's teachers worked for free, and that she didn't expect him to pay for her organization. Her letters patent arrived in May 1671.

Bourgeoys arrived back at Montreal in August 1672 with seven teachers and five other women who still weren't sure what they wanted to do but were willing to give Bourgeoys's way of life a try. In 1673, she designed a habit, or uniform, for her little group of teachers. It included a simple black dress, similar to those worn by peasant women in Champagne, France; a white-trimmed, black headdress; and a crisp, white, linen necktie. The habit made it easier for people to identify these single women as individuals who lived religious lives dedicated to teaching and helping others.

But Bourgeoys's teachers still weren't nuns. Try as she might, she still couldn't convince church officials that they mustn't be cloistered, and that they were capable of managing their own schools, properties and finances independently. For a poor, single, older woman to disagree with powerful bishops about these matters took a lot of courage, but so had visiting a king preparing for war. Bourgeoys accepted their rejections humbly and politely, but she didn't stop trying to change their minds.

Finally, Bourgeoys's courage and patience won out. On June 24, 1694, one year after she had stepped down as its head, the uncloistered Congregation of Notre Dame received the church's official blessing. She and her sisters made their religious vows the next day. By then, Bourgeoys was in her eighties. She had been serving the people of Ville-Marie for forty-seven years, and her organization had expanded to include a boarding school in Quebec, mission schools for Native girls and a teachers' training school—Canada's first—at Montreal.

On New Year's Eve, 1699, the sister in charge of training new members of the order became very ill. When Bourgeoys heard that the young woman was near death, she prayed to God to take her instead. She didn't want to die, but she felt she had lived a long, good life, and there was so much more the other nun could do for people. The next day, Bourgeoys came down with a terrible fever. That same day, the other nun began to get better.

Bourgeoys died on January 12, 1700. Her funeral procession was the longest Montreal had ever seen. Young and old, rich and poor alike gathered to pay their respects. Many people said she had been a saint. On October 13, 1982, the Catholic Church officially agreed with them and canonized her, or declared her a saint. In Canada, St. Marguerite Bourgeoys's special feast day is January 12, but every day she continues to serve as a powerful role model for women who want to change things for the better.

# Louis de Buade, Comte de Frontenac et de Palluau

## 1622–1698

**M**ANY PEOPLE have named their children after kings, but only a few do so because the king is an old family friend. Louis de Buade de Frontenac was born on May 22, 1622, at Saint-Germain, France. When he was baptized, his godfather was none other than King Louis XIII. His father and the king used to play together when they were boys. Having friends in high places can come in handy sometimes. It would definitely help this baby when he grew up.

Frontenac came from a noble family that had served France's

kings for more than four hundred years. Like his father and grandfather before him, young Louis made a career for himself as a soldier. Seeing his first action when he was just a teenager, he worked his way up to positions of command. He served France bravely and well, and was wounded several times. While commanding a regiment in Italy, he broke his arm very badly and never recovered full use of it.

That happened in 1646. Two years later, Frontenac returned to Paris for a rest. When he wasn't away fighting somewhere, he lived at the king's court, and he lived very well indeed. Unfortunately, he didn't have enough money for all the fancy clothes, good food, grand horses, fine wines and great parties he loved. Before long, he was deeply in debt. Still, the ladies of the court found him charming. In the summer of 1648, one of the most beautiful young women in Paris came under his spell.

By the fall, Anne de La Granges and Frontenac had fallen in love. But her father didn't share her opinion of the young count. He thought Frontenac was just after her money, and he forced Anne to go to a convent to keep her away from him. But it was too late. Louis and Anne had already been married secretly a few weeks earlier. All her father could do then was cut her out of the family fortune.

Being short of funds hadn't stopped Frontenac from doing what he wanted before he was married, however, and it didn't stop him afterwards. He and his wife lived like millionaires at the court and the bills kept piling up. They had a baby boy, François-Louis, who was cared for by a village nurse. But soon after their son's birth, Frontenac's wife moved away for a few years, linking up with a group that had different political connections at court than Frontenac did. Their marriage became something of an on-again, off-again affair.

Frontenac saw more military service over the next several

years, but no command in the army paid nearly enough to get him out of debt. The people to whom he owed money were getting rather annoyed. Just in time, King Louis XIV, his godfather's son, came up with a job that would give Frontenac protection from his creditors and a chance to make a living too. He appointed Frontenac the next governor-general of New France.

Frontenac sailed for Quebec without his wife at the end of June 1672. He was supposed to be in charge of military affairs and defence of the colony. Normally, an intendant, or chief administrator, was responsible for justice and for running the financial affairs. A council appointed by the governor and bishop helped make decisions about what should be done, and all important decisions needed royal approval. But Intendant Jean Talon hadn't been replaced yet, so Frontenac started acting as the administrator too. That upset the sovereign council.

Frontenac also upset François-Marie Perrot, the governor of Montreal, by building a new fort on Lake Ontario at what is now Kingston. Frontenac liked the location from a military point of view. He also figured that Native hunters from around the lake would prefer to bring their beaver pelts there instead of canoeing all the way up to Montreal. That's exactly what they started doing when Fort Cataraqui, later renamed Fort Frontenac, was built in 1673.

Perrot was angry. It had been bad enough when Frontenac ordered a group of unpaid habitants from Montreal to go with him to build the fort. Now the fort that Montrealers had helped build was cutting into their fur-trading business. Perrot himself was involved in the business on the side, and his profits were shrinking too.

Complaints about Frontenac's fort reached the king and Jean-Baptiste Colbert, his minister in charge of New France. At first they too were upset. Frontenac's instructions had been to encourage settlement in places where the French already were, not to expand into new areas. But Fort Frontenac did offer protection against enemy forces that might try to come down the St. Lawrence from Lake Ontario. Besides, more furs meant more money for the royal treasury and for wealthy merchants in France, as well as in New France.

Frontenac got off with a warning to be more diplomatic and a reminder that he had to do something to control the *coureurs de bois* (runners of the woods). That was the name given to men who headed west to trade with Native hunters in their home territory. They saved the Natives a trip by bringing their pelts back to the various forts themselves, but then they charged more for the furs than the Natives would have done. There was more excitement to be had and more money to be made as a *coureur de bois* than as a farmer, miller or carpenter. Even some of the soldiers sent to protect New France were taking to the woods.

Montreal was home base for many of the *coureurs de bois,* so Frontenac ordered Perrot to start controlling their activities. When Perrot ignored Frontenac, Frontenac had him arrested. He also arrested a Montreal priest who spoke out against him. Again complaints about Frontenac's actions reached France, and again the king told him he had to find better ways to deal with problems.

But problems kept coming, and Frontenac kept having trouble dealing with them. When Bishop François de Laval (see p. 87) told fur traders to stop supplying Native people with alcohol, Frontenac said Laval was just trying to get more power for church officials. He didn't get along with the new intendant either, and even went so far as to arrest his son for not showing him enough respect. Frontenac also refused to act when council members asked him to do something about the increasing number of Iroquois attacks on French settlers and fur traders.

More and more complaints about Frontenac reached Paris. In

1682, King Louis XIV and Colbert decided that, friend or not, Frontenac would have to be recalled to France. But after his next two replacements wore themselves out trying to cope with New France's problems, the short-tempered Frontenac didn't look so bad. A return to Quebec looked good to Frontenac too. He'd lost much of what he owned because of bad debts, and the bills were still mounting. In 1689, he asked for and received a second appointment as governor.

A serious challenge awaited the sixty-seven-year-old Frontenac back in Canada. The Iroquois were at war again with the French and their Native allies, and England was at war with France too. When Frontenac returned to Quebec, he organized attacks on some New England villages in the hope of cutting off British supplies to the Iroquois. The British colonists decided to fight back. In October 1690, a fleet of more than thirty ships commanded by Sir William Phips sailed from Boston for Quebec.

Phips was sure the French would surrender Quebec when faced with so many troops and boats. That's what had happened when he showed up at Port-Royal (Nova Scotia) in the spring. But Frontenac had no intention of giving up his colony. When he heard that Phips was on the way, he rushed back from Montreal, bringing with him all available troops.

On October 17, Phips sent an officer ashore to tell Frontenac he was bound to lose. The officer was brought, blindfolded, to the governor. When his blindfold was removed, the man found himself face to face with a confident, finely dressed Frontenac surrounded by brightly uniformed military commanders. Frontenac listened politely to Phips's demands for surrender, then told the officer that his only answer to those demands would come from the mouths of his cannons and muskets.

The officer reported back to Phips that Frontenac was ready for any attack and in no mood to surrender. After a few days of sporadic fighting, Phips decided that the smart thing to do was sail back home. He had no idea how long Quebec could hold out, and he didn't want to get trapped in the St. Lawrence when it started to freeze over.

This victory over the British was Frontenac's finest moment in Quebec. In the years that followed, he eventually managed to bring the Iroquois to a point where they were asking for peace talks. But he let the fur trade expand so much that there were more beaver pelts than merchants wanted to buy, and prices plummeted. As well, he often had serious run-ins with the intendant and the sovereign council, and even went so far as to ignore direct orders from the king to change his ways.

Once again, the king and Colbert decided that something had to be done about Frontenac. But the governor didn't have to suffer the humiliation of a second recall. In the fall of 1698, before he could be replaced, Frontenac became very ill. On November 28, he died peacefully in his bed. The funeral was a fine affair. The old soldier would have approved.

# Jean de Brébeuf
## 1593–1649

JEAN DE BRÉBEUF knew that death was near. The tall, grey-haired priest had often seen its dark, ghostly figure in his dreams. He had also seen what the Iroquois did to prisoners like him and Gabriel Lalemant, the small, frail man near him on the raised platform. He hoped the end would come quickly for his friend, but that was not meant to be. Brébeuf's agony would last four hours, but it would take Lalemant eleven hours to die.

In a way, the fate of Brébeuf and many others who fell into the hands of the Iroquois had been sealed nearly forty years earlier when Samuel de Champlain (see p. 27), the founder of Quebec, had decided to side with the Huron against their enemies. From Champlain's point of view, it had been the right thing for the French to do. The Huron were friendly, and they were willing to help him explore new territory. They also had many valuable furs to trade.

But their enemies were the Iroquois, and Champlain's decision made them his enemies too. As more settlers moved into the St. Lawrence, the Iroquois' resentment grew. They didn't like being cut off from the valuable fur trade with the French. The presence of the French, armed with muskets and cannons, was also making it harder for them to beat the Huron and take over their territory. By the time Brébeuf arrived in New France in 1625, attacks by Iroquois war parties were on the rise.

Before then, Brébeuf had been teaching at a college in France and performing his duties as a Roman Catholic priest. But other than his birthdate—March 25, 1593, in Normandy—little else is known of him until he joined the Jesuit religious order at age twenty-four.

The Jesuits were a well-educated and highly respected group with a reputation as the best teachers in Europe. They were also very strongly committed to their Christian faith. That's why Cardinal Richelieu of France wanted them to go to New France. He wanted them to work with Native people there and teach them about Christianity so that they would convert, that is, become Christians. As Christians, they would share many of the same values as the French settlers, and be more likely to accept the French way of life. They would also, from the Church's point of view, be much better off spiritually.

Brébeuf was among the first group of Jesuits sent to New France. He sailed from Dieppe in April 1625 with two other priests, Charles Lalemant and Enemond Massé. Their first year in Canada, they stayed with the Récollets, an order of priests who had come to Quebec ten years earlier. Brébeuf was eager to get to know the Native people in the area, so he spent most of that first fall and winter with a group of Montagnais camped near Quebec.

He lived as they did, and learned to speak Algonquian, the language spoken by the Montagnais, Algonquin and several other Native peoples living north of the St. Lawrence.

The next spring Brébeuf was sent to do missionary work in the *pays des Hurons*, or land of the Huron, around Georgian Bay. Brébeuf was a strong, muscular man, but even for him the trip there was a challenge. He, Father Anne de Noué, and some Huron guides had to paddle supply-laden canoes up the St. Lawrence, Ottawa and Mattawa rivers, across Lake Nipissing and down the French River into Georgian Bay. On this 1,400-kilometre journey, Brébeuf got his first taste of what it was like to paddle day after day through choking swarms of hungry mosquitoes and blackflies, and to carry, or portage, a heavy load around foaming rapids and waterfalls.

Brébeuf and de Noué went to live at a place called Toanché, just north of what is now Penetanguishene. There, Brébeuf learned Iroquoian, the language the Huron shared with members of the Iroquois Confederacy and other nations living south of the St. Lawrence. De Noué found life there very difficult, and in the spring of 1627 he returned to Quebec. Brébeuf stayed in the area for three years, travelling to other Huron villages and earning the respect of the people he visited. They found him to be a wise, kind and thoughtful man. They were also very impressed with his great height and strength.

In 1629, Brébeuf got word to return to Quebec immediately because Champlain was about to surrender New France to British attackers led by David Kirke. After the surrender, Brébeuf went back to working at a college in France. But three years later, Britain ordered the Kirke brothers to give the colony back to France, and in 1633 Brébeuf sailed for Quebec a second time. A few weeks after he arrived, he was sent back into Huron country with instructions to start a permanent mission there.

Brébeuf chose to build his mission, called Saint-Louis, at a small Huron village a few kilometres west of Toanché. Four years later, he built a Jesuit residence on the northeast coast of Nottawasaga Bay, and in 1638 he started another mission about 50 kilometres south of Midland. As new priests arrived, he taught them to speak Iroquoian, and asked them to help him collect new words and expressions used by the Huron so he could put together a Huron dictionary and write down the grammar rules of the language. He translated some prayers and hymns into Iroquoian, and wrote some new ones, too. One hymn, "The Huron Carol," which he wrote and set to the tune of a French folk song, is still sung at Christmas today. He also wrote the Jesuits' annual reports for 1635 and 1636, describing Huron life at the time in great detail. These reports, and those for other years, were known as the *Jesuit Relations*. They were widely read when they were published in France, and helped attract both volunteers and money to continue the missionary efforts.

But these were tragic times for the Huron and dangerous ones for Brébeuf and his fellow priests. Native people were very vulnerable to diseases such as smallpox, measles and flu that Europeans carried to the New World. In the 1630s, three different epidemics claimed as many as 18,000 of the 25,000 to 30,000 Huron living in the area. Their medicine men, already upset with the Jesuits for meddling in the spiritual affairs of their people, claimed that the black-robed priests were evil witch doctors whose spells had brought all the sickness and death. Frightened and angry, people turned against the Jesuits, damaging their small chapels, beating some of them and threatening all of them with death. Most of the Huron who were thinking about becoming Christians changed their minds, and the few dozen who had done so were harassed as much as the priests.

After meeting to talk about what they should do, the Jesuits decided to build a large fortified mission on the Wye River at what is now Midland, Ontario. Inside, French and Christian Huron alike would be safe from both angry Hurons and warring Iroquois who were threatening to send raiding parties into Huron country. Father Isaac Jogues was put in charge of building the new mission, known as Sainte-Marie, and work on it began in 1639. Complete with a church, hospital, blacksmith's shop, bakery, gardens and a large Huron longhouse, it would serve as the Jesuits' headquarters in the region for the next ten years.

Brébeuf left Sainte-Marie in October 1640 to spend the winter visiting people of the Neutral nation, who lived around the western end of Lake Ontario. But the rumours about disease-causing spells had reached that far south, and he was not well received. To make matters worse, in March 1641 he fell on the ice and broke his collarbone, and had to return to Quebec for treatment. There, he was put to work gathering and arranging transportation of shipments of supplies for the Huron missions. After three years of doing that, he returned to his missionary work around Georgian Bay.

By then, the Mohawk (one of the Iroquois nations) were waging a full-scale war against the French living along the St. Lawrence. In October 1646, they killed Isaac Jogues while he was on a peace mission in what's now the state of New York. Four years earlier, he had been captured while bringing a shipment of supplies to Sainte-Marie, and he had been tortured and then held prisoner for more than a year.

By 1647, things were so bad that the Huron were afraid to make their yearly fur-trading trip to Quebec. There were constant Iroquois attacks along the St. Lawrence, and war parties were moving into the *pays des Hurons*. In July 1648, another priest, Antoine Daniel, was killed. Village after village fell to the Iroquois, and hundreds of Huron were killed or taken prisoner.

On March 16, 1649, more than a thousand Iroquois warriors attacked the Saint-Louis mission in the middle of the night. Brébeuf and Gabriel Lalemant were there at the time. While the Jesuits tended the wounded and prayed with the dying, a brave Huron chief, Étienne Annaotaha, tried to maintain some sort of Huron defence. But his people were horribly outnumbered, and he finally told the two priests to escape to Saint-Marie while they still could. When they refused to leave, he led a small group of terrified survivors to safety at Sainte-Marie.

Brébeuf and Lalemant were captured, along with scores of Huron prisoners, and taken to Saint-Ignace, another village that had been destroyed the day before. It was there that the two priests were put on a platform for all to see. They were stripped naked, horribly mutilated, tortured for hours and finally burned to death. A few days later, after the Iroquois had moved on, their remains were recovered and taken to Saint-Marie for burial.

Three months later, with all hope lost, the Jesuits and Huron at Saint-Marie realized they would have to abandon the site. When everyone was packed and ready to leave for Christian Island, to the west, the priests picked up torches and set the buildings on fire. It was the only way they could make sure that the Iroquois didn't take over the mission and use it as a base from which to carry out more deadly raids. By Christmas, three more missionaries had been killed, and a few months later the Iroquois attacked Christian Island too. The few Jesuits still there, along with three hundred or so Christian Huron, managed to escape and make their way back to Quebec, but the proud Huron nation had been totally destroyed.

Nearly three hundred years later, the Jesuits built a large wooden church in Midland, Ontario, opposite the site where Saint-Marie once stood. Known as the Martyrs' Shrine, it was built to honour those Jesuits who had been killed in the service of their God. In June 1930, Pope Pius XI canonized Brébeuf, Lalemant, Daniel, Jogues and two other Jesuits (Charles Garnier and Nöel Chabanel), together with two *donnés,* or laypersons who lived and worked with the Jesuits (René Goupil and Jean de La Lande). These eight, known as the Canadian Martyrs, were North America's first officially recognized saints.

# Louis Jolliet

## 1645–1700

**B**Y THE TIME Louis Jolliet was in his early twenties, his future seemed clear. He was excelling in his studies to become a Jesuit priest, and his musical talents were being recognized in a special way. He'd been chosen as the first organist for the Nôtre-Dame cathedral at Quebec. This was quite an accomplishment for a local boy whose father had been a humble wagon maker and whose mother had been twice-widowed by the time young Jolliet was ten. Many important people agreed that Jolliet, born and educated in the colony, would go far in the church of New France.

Little did they know just how far Jolliet would go, and it wouldn't be as a priest. In 1667, after studying at the Jesuit college for eleven years, Jolliet decided to quit. Usually such a decision meant starting life all over again, without a cent to one's name.

But Quebec's bishop at the time, François de Laval (see p. 84), was a wise and caring man. He loaned Jolliet enough money for a trip to France, where he spent some time thinking about what he wanted to do with his life.

A year later, the young man who loved music, could speak Latin fluently and enjoyed studying mathematics and philosophy was back in Quebec, buying the supplies he needed to start his own business—as a fur trader. There isn't much information about exactly what Jolliet did for the next three years, but he must have done well for himself. If he hadn't, Jean Talon (see p. 90), the intendant (or business manager) of New France, wouldn't have picked him for a special project in 1672.

At the time, colony officials and merchants were still hoping to find a water route to the Pacific that would make trade with the Far East much easier and cheaper than sailing all around the world. One possibility was the Mississippi, a powerful river south of the Great Lakes that Jesuit missionaries had first learned about from many different groups of Native people. Apparently, the river was huge; Natives called it the "father of waters." But which way did it flow—south to the Gulf of Mexico or southwest to California's Pacific coast? Intendant Talon thought Jolliet was the best person to find that out.

Jolliet was pleased that Talon had chosen him, but he would have liked it a lot more if the intendant had come up with the money needed for such a trip. But he hadn't, so Jolliet had to raise the funds himself. To do that, he formed a company with six other men. All seven would pay for the expedition, and they would all share in the profits made from any fur trading they did along the way.

Jolliet set out from Quebec with five of his six partners at the beginning of October 1672. By the first week of December, they had made it all the way to the Jesuit mission at Michilimackinac, where Lakes Michigan and Huron meet. There Jolliet delivered a letter from the head of the Jesuits in Quebec to a priest named Father Jacques Marquette. The letter contained instructions for Marquette to join Jolliet on his journey. When the two men first met, Jolliet may have wondered if it was such a good idea to take the thin, frail-looking priest with him. But as he got to know Marquette better over the winter, he realized that the Jesuit's friendly way with people and his knowledge of six different Native languages would be invaluable.

Jolliet and Marquette, with five other men whose names aren't known, set out in two canoes in mid-May 1673, as soon as the ice had melted. They travelled down Green Bay, along the Fox River and into the Wisconsin River. After paddling about 200 kilometres down the Wisconsin, they reached the Mississippi. On they paddled, often in awe of what they saw—strange new birds, huge herds of buffalo drinking at the water's edge, and large, impressive Native encampments and villages. With Father Marquette interpreting, the French explorers were usually able to convince Native leaders that they meant no harm, and they were treated to warm, generous welcomes in return. Native guides also gave them a lot of information about the mighty river and what lay ahead.

But south of the Ohio River, Jolliet started to get nervous. The Natives there spoke languages Marquette didn't know, and they didn't act very friendly. As well, Jolliet wasn't sure how close they were getting to territory claimed by the Spanish. He still hadn't found the mouth of the Mississippi, but he had seen rivers flowing from the west into the Mississippi, and it was clear that the huge river itself was flowing south to the Gulf of Mexico. He now had the information he had come for, so at some point north of the Arkansas River, he decided they should turn back.

Jolliet had been making detailed maps and notes along the

way, and he did the same thing on the trip back to Lake Michigan via the Illinois River, with a portage to what is now Chicago. He said goodbye to Marquette at Michilimackinac, and spent the winter at Sault Sainte-Marie, carefully copying his maps and notes to leave with the Jesuits there. In May 1674, he set out for home. Just a few kilometres west of Montreal, his canoe overturned. After nearly four hours fighting the rapids, he managed to drag himself ashore, but the three other people with him drowned and his precious maps and notes were lost. He would later learn that his copies had also been lost, in a fire.

Back in Quebec, Jolliet settled back into the life of a successful fur trader, doing business mainly on the north shore of the St. Lawrence. In 1675, he married Claire-Françoise Byssot. He and Byssot would have six children. In 1679, he explored the area of northern Quebec around Hudson Bay. Worried about how the English with the new Hudson's Bay Company were cutting into French-linked fur trading up there, he decided to expand his interests and set up fishing and sealing businesses on Mingan and Anticosti islands in the St. Lawrence. He built a house on Anticosti, and for the next several years spent summers there with his family.

In 1690, on their way up the St. Lawrence to attack Quebec, English forces led by Sir William Phips boarded Jolliet's ship, which was loaded with trade goods and supplies, briefly held his wife hostage and stole everything. Two years later, he suffered another financial loss at the hands of the English. This time they destroyed his business operations on Mingan and Anticosti.

From then on, Jolliet had serious money problems. Nevertheless, in 1694, he explored and mapped the Labrador coast, providing historians with the first detailed accounts of the friendly Inuit people he visited with there. A year later, he was hired to pilot a ship down the St. Lawrence and across the Atlantic to France, and in 1697, back in Quebec, he was named the king's official hydrographer, or waterways expert, in New France.

How and where Jolliet died in 1700 is unknown. What is known is that he spent his last few winters teaching at the Jesuit college he had attended as a boy. His life had come full circle. But on his journey back to his beginnings, the local boy had taken that impressive detour down the mighty Mississippi. He had indeed gone far.

# René-Robert Cavelier de La Salle

## 1643–1687

R ENÉ-ROBERT CAVELIER DE LA SALLE was born in 1643 near Rouen, France. At that time, New France was having a difficult time attracting settlers. The winters there were terrible, the colony often ran low on supplies and Iroquois warriors regularly attacked their French and Huron enemies.

Twenty-four years later, while the New England colonies were beginning to thrive, New France was still struggling to survive. Nevertheless, young La Salle did what few were doing at the time. In 1667, he bought a ticket on a ship bound for Quebec and sailed off in search of grand adventures and glory.

Such a move would not have surprised his Jesuit teachers. Both at the college in Rouen and then at the Jesuit seminary in Paris where he studied for the priesthood, La Salle was considered a bit of a handful. He wasn't rude or disruptive, and when he put his mind to it, he did excellent work. But more often than not, he found school boring and had a hard time sticking to the strict routines Jesuit students were expected to follow. He was always eager to learn something new, but he was never quite sure what he wanted to do. Sensing that he might not be the best candidate for religious life, his superiors delayed his progress towards taking final vows. La Salle finally came to the same conclusion in 1667, when he left the Jesuits and sailed for New France.

La Salle went to Montreal, where his brother, who had become a priest, was working as a teacher. Fortunately for La Salle, members of his brother's religious order, the Sulpicians, were delighted to have a new settler in the small island colony. They gave him a piece of land at the southern end of the island. Right away he built a small fort there and opened up a trading post.

But it didn't take long for La Salle's interests to turn elsewhere. He started learning several Native languages, and then he began asking questions about a great river some Natives called "Ohio" (beautiful water) and others called "Mississippi" (father of waters). Could this great river be the elusive water route across the continent to China? La Salle became so obsessed with finding the route that his neighbours called his land *la Chine,* or China.

In 1669, La Salle got permission from New France's governor, Rémy de Courcelle, to search for that western waterway south of the Great Lakes. But La Salle wasn't about to set off with one or two canoes, as other explorers had. He had grand plans for his expedition, grander than his finances would permit. To raise money, he sold most of his land at Lachine back to the Sulpicians. Then he hired fourteen men and set off from Montreal in July with nine canoes loaded down with supplies.

True to his nature, La Salle didn't take the standard route out of Montreal—up the Ottawa River, over to Lake Nipissing and then west or south. Instead, he paddled straight up the St. Lawrence. By August 2, he had reached Lake Ontario, but a month later, near what's now Hamilton, Ontario, he got sick. When he felt strong enough to travel again, he announced that the trip was off and told his men he was going back to Montreal. No one is sure where he went next. But if La Salle had discovered the Ohio River or Mississippi River shortly after that, as some have claimed, surely he would have shouted the news from the rooftops. In fact, he kept a very low profile when he showed up in Quebec in August 1670 and in Montreal in 1671.

In 1674, La Salle's support for the colony's new governor, Frontenac (see p. 56), paid off in a big way. Frontenac arranged for La Salle to take over a new fort on Lake Ontario, Fort Cataraqui (now Kingston). The fort was in an ideal location because local Native hunters found it much easier to trade their furs there than to take them all the way to Montreal. It was bound to be a real money-maker for La Salle. He renamed it Fort Frontenac in honour of the governor.

But before long, La Salle started working on another grand plan. First he got permission to build two more forts—at Niagara, between Lakes Erie and Ontario, and at Michilimackinac, where Lakes Huron, Superior and Michigan nearly meet. Then he got permission from the king to control any other trading posts he might build when he went exploring in the unclaimed territory bounded by New France, Florida and Mexico.

Obviously, La Salle still wanted to find the Mississippi, but he didn't intend to lose money looking for it this time. The network of forts he would build along the way would make him a major player in the fur-trading business. But he figured it would take more than canoes to move all those furs closer to markets in the east. He decided that he needed a ship that would sail back and forth between Lakes Michigan and Erie. He couldn't just go out and buy one, however. The only way to get a big boat past Niagara Falls was to build it above the falls, and that's exactly what he did.

In the fall of 1678, La Salle sent some of his men ahead with loads of ship parts and building supplies to the southern end of Lake Ontario. There they spent days hauling materials, including seven cannons, up rocky cliffs and around the falls. Then they began building the ship on the Lake Erie side of the Niagara River. By January it was nearly done and work had begun on the new fort. La Salle had to hike back to Montreal in February to deal with a financial mess, but in the spring he returned with more supplies.

On August 7, 1679, a very proud La Salle launched the *Griffon*. Less than a month later, he sailed into Green Bay. He unloaded all the supplies he needed and sent the *Griffon* back with a load of furs. But he would never see the boat again. Not only was it the first ship ever to sail the Great Lakes, but it also appears to have been the lakes' first shipwreck.

La Salle's next two years might have driven other men mad. Some thought La Salle must have been crazy in the first place to do what he did. With fourteen men in four canoes he paddled down Lake Michigan in stormy autumn weather, built a small fort, moved on to the Illinois River and, in January 1680, built another fort at what is now Peoria, Illinois. After sending some men on ahead, he made a trouble-ridden trek back to Fort Niagara, desperate to find out where the *Griffon* was. In April, he found Fort Frontenac burned to the ground and learned that one of his supply ships had sunk in the St. Lawrence. He raced to Montreal to deal with his money problems, rushed back to Fort Frontenac and then headed on to Michilimackinac and the Illinois River.

But the fort La Salle had built there had also burned down, and his men were nowhere to be found. Back he went to

Michilimackinac, where he learned the likely fate of the *Griffon*. Then he was off to Montreal again, in the summer of 1681. Just before Christmas, he finally met up with his missing men at the southern end of Lake Michigan. Then he set off with eighteen Natives and twenty-three Frenchmen, hauling his canoes on sleds down the frozen Illinois River.

La Salle reached his great river on February 6, 1682. By then he knew that the Mississippi didn't flow west. Another explorer, Louis Jolliet (see p. 69), had found that out a few years earlier. But no European had travelled the length of it yet. That spring, La Salle did. He reached the mouth on April 7. On August 9, 1682, wearing a scarlet cloak he took everywhere, he claimed all the new territory he had explored for King Louis XIV and France. He named the territory Louisiana in the king's honour.

Two years later, La Salle made another trip to Louisiana. It would be his last. To raise enough money and royal support for a grand scheme to settle the area, he joined forces with Abbé Claude Bernou. Bernou was a power-hungry priest who wanted to become bishop in a settlement he hoped to start on the Gulf of Mexico, at the mouth of the Rio Grande. By changing his maps a little, La Salle was able to convince the king that both he and Bernou wanted to go to the same area, and the king finally approved a combined expedition.

Plans for this trip were even grander than any La Salle could have imagined, and things got out of hand. Soon the group included at least three hundred settlers, several of whom were women and children; one hundred soldiers; and three overloaded boats. There were fights over who was in charge, and their exact destination wasn't clear. The doomed expedition finally sailed from France in July 1684.

Three years later, a pitiful, desperate La Salle was still haunting the Gulf coast, searching for the mouth of the Mississippi.

Disease had claimed many of the settlers, and of the 180 people still with him in 1685, in 1687 only twenty-five remained at the small fort he had built near what is now Galveston, Texas. In January 1687, La Salle left the fort on foot, heading northeast in search of the Illinois River that would take him home.

Two months later, all of La Salle's grand schemes were finally put to rest. A few of his men had had enough of their red-cloaked leader. On the morning of March 19, 1687, one of them shot him in the head. One hundred and sixteen years later, the United States paid Napoleon $15 million for the Louisiana territory that La Salle had explored and claimed for France.

# Kateri Tekakwitha
## 1656–1680

KATERI TEKAKWITHA was born in the Mohawk River Valley in what is now New York State. Her father was a Mohawk warrior who had taken a Christian Algonquin woman as his wife. Long before Europeans arrived in North America, the Mohawk, together with the Oneida, Onondaga, Cayuga and Seneca, had decided to stop fighting each other and form the Five Nations, or Iroquois Confederacy.

When the French, Dutch and English started to move into Iroquois territory, warriors belonging to that confederacy, or alliance, fought back. And when other Native peoples, such as the Huron and Algonquin, began trading furs with the French, Iroquois warriors attacked them too. By the time Tekakwitha was born, Mohawks from her village were often among those war parties that travelled up to Montreal to attack new settlements along the St. Lawrence.

But the Europeans brought with them something the Mohawk and other Native peoples couldn't fight, and that was smallpox, a terribly infectious disease. When Kateri Tekakwitha was just four years old, a smallpox epidemic struck her village. People came down with burning fevers, and scabby sores covered their bodies. Tekakwitha's mother, father and young brother were among those who died. Tekakwitha survived, but she was left with damaged eyesight and deep scars on her face.

Tekakwitha's uncle, the village chief, adopted her, but she did not have an easy life. Other youngsters often made fun of her because of the way she looked and because she couldn't see very well. When she was ten, news reached her village that King Louis XIV was sending a French force of more than a thousand men to wipe out Native villages in the Mohawk Valley. People in Tekakwitha's village and three others managed to hide before the troops arrived from Quebec, but all their lodges, crops and supplies were burned.

The Mohawk rebuilt their villages and reluctantly made peace with the French. They also asked that some Jesuit missionaries be sent to their valley. When the first group of missionaries arrived for a three-day visit in the fall of 1667, Tekakwitha was given the job of running errands for them and bringing them food. The black-robed Catholic priests treated her politely and with respect, and that meant a lot to her.

Tekakwitha became very interested in their religion. The more she learned about it, the more she tried to follow its beliefs. Eventually, she decided that she would be able to live a holier life if she remained single, like the Catholic nuns she'd heard about from Christian Algonquins and Hurons living in her village. This decision caused her a lot of trouble. All Mohawk girls were expected to get married. Her relatives got angry with her when she resisted pressure to do so, especially when she turned down a young warrior they had chosen to be her husband.

More people became angry with Tekakwitha when she chose to become a Christian and was baptized on Easter Sunday in 1676. Mohawks who didn't want to lose their own way of life felt betrayed. Several of them began treating her like a slave. They teased her mercilessly, made her carry very heavy loads and wouldn't give her enough to eat. Some people even threatened to kill her. Finally some friends and relatives helped her escape and go to live with them at Caughnawaga (Kahnawake), near Montreal.

There Tekakwitha was free to live the holy life she had longed for. She prayed often, attended all the religious services the Jesuits held in the village, and did everything she could to help anyone in need. After a visit with teaching and nursing sisters working in Montreal, she began to hope that she might be able to start an order of nuns for Native women, who would then teach and nurse in their own villages.

But that hope would not become a reality. Tekakwitha had never been very strong. Still, she always worked hard and often fasted, or did without food, as a form of self-discipline. But the harder she pushed herself, the weaker she became. A year or so after her visit to Montreal, she became very ill, and by Easter week, 1680, it was clear to those taking care of her that she was dying.

On April 17, when she was only twenty-four years old, Tekakwitha died peacefully, her last words a prayer. Then something very unusual happened. All the smallpox scars and the strain of illness disappeared from Tekakwitha's face. Those who witnessed this transformation took it as a sign of how much God must have loved her. As villagers passed by her open coffin and saw how beautiful she looked, many said the change was miraculous.

Word of the miracle spread quickly. Because of the pure and holy life she had led, Tekakwitha became known as the Lily of the Mohawks. Some people began praying to her to ask God for help in times of trouble, and reports of miraculous cures reached church officials in Quebec. Eventually, a shrine was built in her memory at Caughnawaga, and many people came there to pray.

In 1943 the Catholic Church officially recognized what a good life Tekakwitha had led. That year she was declared venerable, a term meaning very holy and worthy of respect. In 1980, Pope John Paul II held a special ceremony to beatify her, or declare her blessed. This was the church's way of saying that she must surely be in heaven. The good and gentle Lily of the Mohawks was the first Native person to be beatified.

More than three hundred years after her death, many Canadian and American Catholics still continue to pray to Blessed Kateri Tekakwitha for spiritual strength and guidance.

# François de Laval
## 1623–1708

NEW FRANCE was run in much the same way as France and most other European countries had been since the Middle Ages. Society was organized like a pyramid, with the king and his representatives, the governor-general and the local governors, at the top. Beneath the king in position and power were nobles and wealthy friends, who were granted large sections of land. They were known as seigneurs. At the bottom of the pyramid were merchants, tradespeople and the settlers who rented and farmed the seigneurs' lands, or seigneuries.

And just as popes and bishops often had as much power as kings and nobles in the Middle Ages, church authorities were still seen as belonging near the top of the pyramid in French society in the seventeenth century. The king of France knew that missionary work played an important part in settling a new colony, and he gave religious orders such as the Jesuits and Récollets seigneuries too. Priests and nuns alike built chapels, churches, schools and hospitals, and their orders became major property holders in the new settlements.

At first, bishops in France were in charge of church-related matters in New France. However, in the 1650s, the king and the pope began to discuss the possibility of giving the colony its very own bishop. There were arguments over who should get the job and whether he would be loyal first to Rome or to the king, but in 1658 an agreement was finally reached. François de Laval was to become the first bishop of all of New France.

Laval came from one of the oldest noble families of France. Born in 1623 near the city of Chartres, he was enrolled in studies leading to the priesthood by the time he was eight years old. He attended a Jesuit college for ten years, and impressed his teachers with how smart, honest and sincere he was. Not long before he was to become a priest, his widowed mother asked him to come home and be the head of the family because his two older brothers had been killed in battle.

Laval went home to help out his mother, but after a year he felt he had to return to the religious life he had chosen for himself. He was ordained to the priesthood in 1647, and immediately began teaching orphans and taking care of the sick in the Normandy diocese of Évreux, where his uncle was the bishop. A year later, when he was just twenty-five, he was made the archdeacon of Évreux, a job that had him managing the affairs of more than 150 parishes. He handled his duties superbly, and still found time to personally care for the sick and the poor.

By the time he was asked about becoming the bishop of New France, Laval was seriously considering going as a missionary to the Far East, where he thought he could help more people in need. Instead, in 1658, he found himself at the centre of some messy politics and power struggles over who should get the bishop's job. His consecration as bishop in December 1658 was held in secret so that the Abbé de Queylus, head of the Sulpicians in Montreal, wouldn't find out about it until after the fact. De Queylus had wanted to be the bishop, and he was bound to cause trouble when he heard about Laval's appointment.

Laval sailed for New France in April 1659, and arrived at Quebec in mid-June. Sure enough, de Queylus objected strongly when he learned that Laval would have authority over him. But Laval calmly informed him that that was what the pope and the king wanted, and until they changed their minds, that was the way things would be. Then Laval set about seeing how he might best care for his new flock.

There were still fewer than three thousand people in New France when Laval arrived. Settlers lived in fear of Iroquois attacks; supplies were often slow to arrive from France; and people needed schools, hospitals, jobs and farms. As well, the sale and trade of alcohol was causing serious trouble, especially for Aboriginal people. The fiery French brandy had a very powerful effect on Native drinkers. When they were drunk, it was easier to cheat them out of their furs. Drunkenness also led to the abuse of women and children. Right away, the new bishop began looking for ways the church could help solve some of these problems.

But before long, Laval got caught up in petty arguments over what should be done and who should do it. Like Abbé de Queylus, Governor Pierre de Voyer d'Argenson didn't like the idea of having Laval telling him what to do. When Laval said governors could no longer hold the honorary position of church warden and sit in the warden's special seat near the altar, d'Argenson became very angry. He said Laval wasn't showing him the respect he deserved. When the bishop tried to get him to ban the brandy trade with Natives, he told him to stop interfering in government business.

D'Argenson complained to the king that Laval was too bossy and wouldn't listen to anyone else's opinions. In 1661, fed up, he asked to be replaced and returned to France. At first, his replacement, Governor Pierre Dubois Davaugour, got along with Laval. By then, Louis XIV had reorganized how New France was run, and the bishop was given a place on the new sovereign council with the governor and intendant, or manager of the colony. From that position of power, Laval pushed for a halt to the liquor trade, and Davaugour finally agreed.

Most traders, merchants and seigneurs argued against a ban. They said that Native hunters would just start taking their furs to Dutch and English traders and getting whisky from them. But Laval announced that anyone caught selling alcohol to Natives would be excommunicated, or refused baptism, marriage, communion and the other sacraments of the Catholic Church. This most serious religious punishment, together with the governor's threat of prison time and even execution, dried up most alcohol trafficking for about five years.

However, in 1668, Intendant Jean Talon (see p. 90) talked the sovereign council into lifting the ban and making Native drunkenness illegal instead. Laval failed in his fight to reverse this unfair decision. All he could do was make it clear that the Church still saw alcohol trading as a mortal, or very serious, sin. Ten years later, in 1678, the governing council did agree to restrict the legal sale or trading of alcohol to French settlements only. But Laval knew that once the fur traders left the settlements, there'd be no way to stop them from doing whatever they wanted with the kegs of legally-bought brandy loading down their large canoes. Business interests would win out in the end.

Laval had to fight a few battles to bring about changes in how the Church was run too. He approved of the good work being done by priests belonging to religious orders such as the Jesuits and Récollets, but he also wanted to give the colony many well-trained parish priests. In 1663, he opened a seminary where young men could receive training in Canada to prepare them to meet the needs of local settlers. Priests who studied and were ordained there were under the control of the bishop. That way, Laval could decide where they went and could move them if they weren't doing a good job. The seminary would eventually grow into the University of Laval.

Laval had some run-ins with governors over the years about how money should be raised to support parish priests and local churches. He also had some difficulties trying to figure out how much independence some of the orders of nuns working in New France should have in managing their own convents, schools and hospitals. But even if he was difficult to get along with at times, everyone agreed that the new bishop was an incredibly holy, kind and generous man.

From the day he arrived, Laval lived very simply. He wore his clothes until they couldn't be mended any more, and gave away the money he was supposed to spend on himself. Even though he was the bishop, he got up before dawn every morning to open the church, ring the bells and celebrate the first Masses of the day. He nursed the sick and fed the hungry. He visited every parish at least once a year, and listened to the needs of his people, non-Native and Native alike. Even when he was old and weak, he continued to serve them. He suffered most of his life from painful, swollen veins in his legs, and when he could barely stand any more, he humbly accepted piggyback rides to the church.

In the early 1680s, with his health failing, Laval told the king and Rome that it was time to think about finding his replacement. A new bishop, Abbé Jean-Baptiste de La Croix de Saint-Vallier, was chosen in 1685, but wasn't officially consecrated until 1688. Laval then retired to his seminary to spend his last years helping others. He was deeply hurt when the new bishop reduced the seminary from being the control centre for all parishes in New France to simply a training school for new priests, and he was very sad when fire reduced the seminary to ashes in 1701 and again in 1705.

But Laval humbly accepted the changes Saint-Vallier brought in, and when Saint-Vallier was in France for several years, Laval performed many of the bishop's duties without complaint. However, time and poor health finally took their toll. The entire colony went into mourning when Canada's first bishop died on May 6, 1708. He had devoted nearly fifty years of his life to the people of New France and, like all great leaders, had expected no more from them than he demanded of himself. He practised what he preached until the day he died.

# Jean Talon
## 1625?–1694

SOMETHING HAD to be done about New France. France's king, Louis XIV, knew that. So did Jean-Baptiste Colbert, his new minister in charge of the Canadian colony. Few people were settling there, the land wasn't being cleared, supplies were always running low and relations with the Iroquois nations were anything but peaceful. It was already 1663, more than fifty years since Samuel de Champlain (see p. 27) had founded Quebec, and things seemed to be getting worse each year. The time had come to change the way the colony was run.

The first thing the king did was to make New France a royal province. That meant taking back the fur-trade monopoly from a group of businessmen known as the Company of One Hundred Associates. In exchange for total control over the fur trade, the associates had promised to bring over new farmers and skilled tradesmen, help them get settled in the colony, and make sure needed supplies arrived each spring and summer. Instead, they had kept most of the profits for themselves and done very little to help the colony.

Then King Louis and Colbert set up a new royal, or sovereign, council headed by the governor-general, a bishop and an intendant, or administrator, plus five councillors. The governor was now to focus mainly on military matters, especially defence, and on foreign affairs, or dealings with other countries. The bishop was to be responsible for the spiritual well-being of the colony and for any church-related business. The intendant was to deal with the justice system, population growth, expansion, trade, supplies, transportation, policing, spending royal funds and pretty much anything else that came up. The king and Colbert decided to ask a man named Jean Talon to take on this last job.

For most people it would have been an impossible mission. But Talon, like an expert juggler, was already used to keeping track of many things at once. Born in the province of Champagne, France, he had received an excellent education at a Jesuit school in Paris. When he finished school, he took a job as commissary for the French army. As such, he was in charge of getting and distributing the food and supplies the soldiers needed. He did that job so well that in 1655 he was appointed administrator, or intendant, of the entire French province of Hainault.

By the time the king and Colbert called on him to help out in New France, Talon had earned a reputation as a very honest, capable man with a superb business sense. They were both very pleased when the forty-year-old bachelor agreed to go to Quebec. In March 1665, the king made it official, appointing Talon as the first intendant of Canada, Acadia, Newfoundland and any other French colonies in North America.

Talon landed at Quebec in September 1665. A few months earlier, an entire French regiment had arrived to protect the colony from warring Iroquois. The king had agreed that when the military campaign was over, soldiers from the regiment would be allowed to stay in New France if they wanted to. The king had also sent across some more *filles du roi*, single women interested in getting married. Talon could see that there was a good chance a lot of new couples would soon be looking for places to live.

So one of the first things the new intendant did was to reclaim some land near Quebec that the Jesuits weren't using. Then he came up with plans to build forty new houses on three clusters of pie-shaped lots. The houses would be close together in the middle so the settlers could help each other out, and their farms would fan out behind their homes.

To get the project started, Talon bought the first house himself. As others were finished, new settlers moved in. Talon gave them tools, seeds and food to tide them over until they harvested their first crops. In exchange, they promised to clear about one hectare of their own land and a hectare on a new section where no one was living yet. The small-scale building boom was a great success.

At the same time, Talon also set up several new courts to deal with a backlog of legal problems. To save everybody time and money, he also encouraged a lot of people to settle their differences out of court. Then he turned his attention to finding more jobs for people and helping the colony produce more of the supplies it needed.

Once more, Talon took the lead. For example, when he started up a ship-building business at Quebec, he ordered and paid for the first ship himself and talked the king into buying the second one. When he got the first tanneries up and running to make leather from hides, he ordered made-in-Canada shoes for the soldiers. Soon there were new jobs for both tanners and shoemakers.

Talon encouraged settlers to plant new crops, such as hemp, barley and hops. Hemp could be used to make rope for sails, and to make sacking and other rough cloth. To pressure farmers into growing it, he collected all the thread that was for sale in the colony and announced that there was now only one way to "buy" it—by trading hemp for it. If you needed to sew new clothes, curtains and bedding, or mend old ones, you had to grow or buy some hemp.

Talon also put his businessman's mind to work looking for ways to cut down on drunkenness in the colony. Most people saw beer as a healthier drink than the potent French brandy that was sold and traded in New France. People didn't get drunk as much on beer either. So Talon built a brewery with his own money. Naturally, he bought the barley and hops he needed from local farmers.

Within a couple of years, new businesses were starting up everywhere, thanks to Talon. It was he who first figured out that the best way to move valuable oak logs from distant forests was to float them down rivers. He gave women looms so they could weave carpets from the wool of sheep raised in the colony. He opened an iron-ore mine, and set up cod and seal fisheries. Within a few years, the colony was actually exporting goods, rather than waiting helplessly for supplies to come to it.

Talon served as intendant from 1665–68 and, after three months back in France, from 1668–72. During that time, New France's population more than doubled, to nearly seventy-five hundred. In 1671 alone, nearly seven hundred babies were born in the colony. With the future looking so rosy, Talon began to encourage exploration to the north, west and south, and also sent people in search of new mineral deposits. He even began plans for a road running all the way to Acadia.

When he returned to France in 1672, Talon continued to give the king advice on what would be best for New France. The king rewarded him for doing such a good job by giving him a very important position at court, and in 1678 he made Talon a count. Talon lived in comfort in Paris for the rest of his life. He died on November 24, 1694.

New France's great intendant died a wealthy man. Sadly, though, New France didn't fare as well. Without his vision, energy and support, almost all the businesses he started were neglected or abandoned. Still, he had planted seeds of hope in the land. The day would come when those seeds would take root and be harvested by the descendants of those people who had once shared his vision.

# Pierre-Esprit Radisson
## 1640–1710

**T**ENSION WAS growing in the small French settlement of Sainte-Marie-de-Gannentaa, north of what is now Syracuse, New York. The Onondaga, one of the five nations of the Iroquois Confederacy, had invited the French Jesuits to build a mission in their territory. But when four of the black-robed priests and three dozen or so volunteers started putting up the fortified settlement in the summer of 1657, the mood of the Iroquois changed. Some members of the confederacy began planning an attack.

As winter set in, so did heart-chilling fear. Word reached the mission that the attack would come in the early spring. To keep their hopes alive, they secretly began building some boats and canoes in which to escape. But they still didn't know how they would make it to the lake when the ice started to melt. There were hundreds of warriors camped nearby, just waiting for them to make a move. It was Pierre Radisson, the youngest volunteer, who figured that move out.

When he was a boy, Radisson had been captured by the Mohawk while he was hunting near his home at Trois-Rivières. The warriors took him to a Mohawk village in upstate New York, where a Native family adopted him. He lived with them for about three years, learning their ways and customs. Twice he tried to escape. The first time, he was caught, brought back to the village and tortured until his adopted family pleaded for his life. The second time, in 1654, he made it to a Dutch settlement, Fort Orange, and was eventually put on a Dutch ship sailing from New York for Europe. He was back home in Trois-Rivières by the fall.

Now Radisson was trying to avoid being captured again. Having lived with the Iroquois, he knew how important feasts were to them and how they felt obligated to accept an invitation to one. So he let the Natives know that the French were having a feast and they were all invited. For days he kept everyone busy preparing all sorts of food just the way the Iroquois liked it. On the chosen afternoon, the French carried the food outside the gate to their waiting guests. After eating and drinking for hours, the Natives fell asleep. When they woke up, the French were gone.

After a close call like this, many people would be happy for the chance to settle down somewhere safe. But not Radisson. He loved adventure, and he could never get enough of the beauty of the Canadian wilderness. The life of a *coureur de bois* was the life for him. He was young, he was strong, and he was eager to spend months paddling a loaded canoe along unexplored rivers and lakes in search of Native hunters willing to trade their catch of beaver pelts. Besides, being a fur trader was a great way to make some money.

When Radisson got back to Trois-Rivières, he met his widowed sister's new husband for the first time. Médard Chouart des Groseilliers shared Radisson's love of adventure and outdoor life, and the two men got along very well. It didn't take them long to start making plans to discover new hunting grounds. But a group of wealthy people in France, the Company of One Hundred Associates, controlled the fur trade in New France. Only people who worked for them, and a chosen few to whom the governor gave licences, could legally trade with the Natives.

Radisson and Groseilliers knew their chances of getting a licence were very slim. Asking for one would tip off officials about what they had in mind, and they would be prevented from going. So, in August 1659, they sneaked off in the middle of the night with a few other *coureurs de bois* who had agreed to join them. They spent that fall and winter in the area south and west of Lake Superior, trading their supply of cloth, beads, tools, food and brandy for some of the finest furs they had ever seen.

The next summer Radisson, Groseilliers and nearly three hundred Natives paddled dozens of canoes down the Ottawa River to Montreal. People cheered when they saw how many furs they had with them. Radisson and Groseilliers wanted to cheer too. They had enough furs to pay for all their trade supplies and have plenty of money to spare. But by the time the governor was finished with them, they were deeply in debt. He confiscated their furs and fined them both for trading without a licence. Furious, Groseilliers sailed to France to ask the king to reverse the governor's decision, but he got nowhere. The king wasn't about to let the profits from that many furs fall into the hands of two rough and ready independent traders.

That rejection in France marked a turning point for Radisson and his brother-in-law. If they couldn't live the life they loved in New France, they would see if England liked their plans to expand the fur trade north to Hudson Bay. The two men found support in New England for a voyage north through Frobisher Strait, but the ship's captain turned back when faced with an obstacle course of icebergs.

Back in New England with few furs and more debt, Radisson and Groseilliers were lucky to meet a very rich English business-man, Sir George Carteret. Always on the lookout for new invest-ments, Carteret convinced them to return to England with him in 1665 to tell King Charles II about their fur-trading plans for the Hudson Bay area. The king was interested in what they had to say, and he sent them to meet his cousin, Prince Rupert, who was running low on money. A fur-trading business might be just what he needed to solve his financial problems.

In June 1668, Prince Rupert arranged for two ships to take Radisson and Groseilliers on a trial run from England to Hudson Bay. Radisson's ship was damaged and had to turn back, but Groseilliers, aboard the *Nonsuch,* made it safely to James Bay. A year later, he returned with a load of furs valuable enough to con-vince Prince Rupert and some of his rich friends to organize a new fur-trading company. The king granted them rights to trade in the area drained by rivers flowing into Hudson Bay, and on May 2, 1670, the Hudson's Bay Company was born.

Once again, though, the two men responsible for getting so many furs were cut out of the profits. Radisson and Groseilliers were not made partners in the Hudson's Bay Company. For the next five years they worked for the company, but they had to fight for every penny they made. In 1675, fed up with the way they were being treated by the English, they sneaked across the English Channel to see what the French were willing to offer them.

Jean-Baptiste Colbert, Louis XIV's minister in charge of New France, talked Radisson and Groseilliers into returning to Quebec to talk to Governor Frontenac (see p. 56) about competing with the English for furs in the north. But Frontenac preferred to support his friend, René-Robert Cavelier de La Salle (see p. 74), in his fur-trading expeditions. Frustrated, Radisson and Groseilliers spent the next few years trying to get back into the fur trade legally, but they failed to do so.

Frontenac turned a blind eye when they organized a trip into Hudson Bay in 1682 to start a competing French settlement at the mouth of the Nelson River. But when they sailed back to Quebec the next spring with a poacher's ship from New England loaded with Hudson's Bay Company furs, the new governor, Joseph de La Barre, couldn't ignore what they had done. The English were bound to be upset. Even though Radisson had just taken what a New Englander had already got illegally, he had also been trying to set up shop in territory claimed by England. What's more, he and Groseilliers had no intention of paying taxes on the ill-gotten furs.

La Barre sent the New England ship back to Boston and Radisson and Groseilliers back to France, where they did not receive a warm welcome. Within months, Groseilliers was back in Trois-Rivières, and in 1684, an annoyed, nearly broke Radisson had slipped back across the English Channel to work for the Hudson's Bay Company again.

It's not known what happened to Groseilliers after that. Radisson, however, kept working for the Hudson's Bay Company until he died. On one trip back to Canada, he confiscated a boatload of furs from a French trading post on Hudson Bay and brought them back to London. After that, he became a wanted man in New France, with a reward offered to anyone who brought him back to Quebec.

Nobody ever collected that reward, but Radisson was never adequately rewarded for his efforts on behalf of the company he played a major part in founding. Twice widowed, he married a third time late in his life, but when he died in 1710, that wife and her three young children were left in poverty.

Radisson spent his last years in noisy, crowded London. He probably would have preferred to grow old at some small trading post beside a river or lake in northern Canada. But that was not to be, and neither was his dream of a great French fur-trading company with claims to the territory around Hudson Bay.

# Pierre Le Moyne d'Iberville
## 1661–1706

EARLY EVERYONE in New France knew Pierre Le Moyne's family. His father, Charles Le Moyne de Longueuil and de Châteauguay, arrived at Quebec in 1641 and came to Montreal in 1646, just four years after its founding. Many people saw him as a hero because of how bravely he fought against attacking Iroquois during the struggling colony's early years. He was also a very successful businessman. He made a fortune in the fur trade, and eventually became the richest man on the island. He owned a house and several company properties on Rue St-Joseph in Montreal, and another home at Longueuil, his seigneury on the south shore of the St. Lawrence.

But over time, Charles Le Moyne and his wife, Catherine Thierry, would be best known as the parents of some very famous sons, the most notable being Pierre d'Iberville (named after Iberville, a tract of land Le Moyne's family held in France). Iberville was the third-oldest of twelve sons and two daughters born to the Le Moynes. As soon as his father let him, he went sailing up and down the St. Lawrence on the family's merchant ships, and by the time he was a teenager he could navigate the river himself. When he was in his late teens, he also received some naval training in France.

Iberville made his grand entrance on history's stage when he was twenty-five. By then, the English had built several Hudson's Bay Company (HBC) forts in the northwest, and Native hunters in the region were taking their furs and pelts to them instead of going all the way to Montreal. Four years earlier, French merchants had formed the Compagnie du Nord to compete with the Hudson's Bay Company, but without their own trading posts on Hudson Bay and James Bay, the French just kept losing more and more business to the English. So in 1686, Compagnie du Nord investors talked Governor Jacques-René de Brisay de Denonville into allowing an expedition to travel north to set up some French forts in Hudson's Bay Company territory, and Iberville was on that expedition.

An officer from France, Pierre de Troyes, was in charge of the thirty French soldiers and seventy French Canadians who set out up the Ottawa River on March 20, but without Pierre and his two brothers, Paul and Jacques, the troops might never have made it to their destination. These three were strong young men, with experience in the ways of the voyageurs, and it was they who kept the rest of the men going through nearly ninety days of paddling and portaging into the northern wilderness. When they finally reached Fort Moose (now Moose Factory), Troyes decided the easiest way to establish a French fort was simply to attack and take over an English one.

The plan worked. Surprised, the English surrendered without much of a fight, but not before Iberville nearly got killed. After the French bashed open the gate, he rushed in waving his sword and aiming his pistol. But the English managed to push back the gate before anyone else could follow him in. Single-handedly, he held off the fort's defenders until his troops battered the gate down again. This was the first of many incidents during his life that would earn Iberville a reputation as one of the bravest fighters Quebec had ever produced.

That summer, the French captured two more Hudson's Bay Company forts. Iberville also captured the ship of the HBC governor, John Bridgar, and took him prisoner for a while. Troyes headed back to Quebec in August, leaving Iberville in charge of the three forts. After a tough winter and spring at Fort Moose, which Iberville renamed Saint-Louis, he gave up waiting for French ships to arrive with supplies and returned to Quebec. Then he sailed for France to drum up more support for the Compagnie du Nord's efforts on Hudson Bay. A year later, he was back at Quebec with a new ship, which he sailed up to James Bay later that summer.

For the next nine years, Iberville fought many battles on behalf of the Compagnie du Nord to try to gain control over the fur trade on and around Hudson Bay. He spent the winter of 1688 on a ship trapped in the frozen Albany River because two cannon-firing English ships wouldn't let him leave with a load of furs. But the English were stuck in the ice too and, after losing many men to scurvy, surrendered to Iberville in the spring. He took another fort, New Severn, in 1690, and forced the English to surrender York Fort in 1694. But winning York cost him the life of his young brother Louis, who was just eighteen. What's more, the English took back the fort, which Iberville had renamed Fort Bourbon, the very next year.

In 1697, on his last trip to Hudson Bay, Iberville gave France one of its greatest victories at sea. Three heavily armed English ships, including the fifty-six-gun Royal Navy frigate *Hampshire,* had trapped his flagship, the *Pelican,* near Hayes River. Other captains might have hoisted a white flag, but not Iberville. He went on the offensive, shouting orders to raise and lower sails and to load and reload his cannons. The four ships battled for nearly three hours. At one point, Iberville dared to sail between the two HBC ships, returning fire to the right and the left as he manoeuvred his way past them. Then he turned around to challenge the *Hampshire* head on.

Iberville sank the *Hampshire* and captured one HBC ship, but the *Pelican* was badly damaged and he and his crew had to abandon it. Just in time, three more French ships arrived with supplies and reinforcements, and after a few more days of fighting, the governor of Hudson Bay gave up York Fort again and surrendered the entire area to the French. Iberville left his brother Joseph to act as governor, and sailed for France that fall, never to return to Hudson Bay or New France again.

Trying to gain control of the Hudson Bay fur trade wasn't all that kept Iberville busy during the 1690s. In 1692, he captured three English supply ships while patrolling the New England coast for Governor Frontenac. Later that year, and again in 1693, he wanted to return to Hudson Bay but had to guard supply ships sailing to New France instead. During that break from fighting battles, he finally married Marie-Thérèse Pollet, a young woman from Quebec whom he'd been seeing for a few years. Pollet and Iberville would have five children, and she would eventually settle on their estate in France.

In 1696, under orders from King Louis's marine minister, Iberville sailed to Newfoundland to attack the English fishing settlements there. But before doing that, he sailed up the Saint John

River to do battle with some English ships that were stopping supplies from getting through to the French settlers at Acadia. He
succeeded in his mission, and captured an English frigate too. He
also took a little detour down to the English fort William Henry,
and captured and destroyed it before leaving for the Grand Banks.

Iberville sailed to French-run Placentia, in Newfoundland,
late in the fall with three ships and a group of tough, experienced
French-Canadian and Native fighters. From there he marched his
men to Ferryland while Placentia's governor, Jacques-François de
Brouillan, sailed there with his French soldiers. When they met
up, they all marched north to launch a surprise attack on St.
John's. The settlement fell on November 30 and was destroyed.
Iberville spent the next four months terrorizing other English
coastal settlements, sneaking up on snowshoes and catching residents off guard. But before he could take the last two English settlements, he had to join his brother Joseph, who had sailed from
France with orders for them to go back to Hudson Bay.

When Iberville left New France for good, he was a rich man.
During those years of fighting, he claimed most of the furs he
confiscated for himself, kept or sold many of the ships he captured, and held many of the prisoners he took for ransom. He also
made a small fortune from fish he confiscated in Newfoundland.
But he wasn't ready yet to settle down. When Louis XIV's advisers
gave him the chance to become an explorer, he jumped at the
opportunity. In October 1698, he and his brother Jean-Baptiste
sailed to the Gulf of Mexico with instructions to find and sail up
the mouth of the Mississippi, something an earlier explorer,
René-Robert Cavelier de La Salle (see p. 74), had tried and failed
to do. Once more, he did what he set out to do. He reached the
Mississippi in March 1699 and built a small fort at what is now
Ocean Springs, Mississippi.

Iberville put his brother in charge there and returned to

France, where the king made him a knight, or chevalier, of the Order of Saint Louis, an honour for bravery never before given to a French Canadian. Over the next three years, he kept pushing French officials to support further exploration and settlement of Louisiana before the English moved west of the Appalachians and took over the Mississippi fur trade. He made two more trips there, in 1700 and 1701, and built two more forts in the area. He also spent time making friendly contacts with Native hunters, encouraging them to bring their furs and pelts to the French forts. He returned to France in 1702 and never made it back to Louisiana. His brother Jean-Baptiste (Le Moyne de Bienville) would eventually become Louisiana's governor and go down in history as the founder of New Orleans.

Iberville was left with a permanent reminder of the time he spent in the semi-tropical Gulf of Mexico—malaria. He was bedridden with chills and soaring fevers many times over the next three years. But in 1706, he felt strong enough to take on one more assignment. He was to drive the English from their settlements in the Caribbean. He took Nevis (St. Kitts) on April 2, capturing nearly seven thousand prisoners and leaving the beautiful island settlement in ruins. Then he prepared to sail northwest and attack Atlantic coastal settlements in the Carolinas. But the great warrior never made it past Cuba. In early July, he caught yellow fever. A few days later, on July 9, he was dead. His body was taken from his ship and buried in Havana.

For many years after his death, Iberville's reputation was under attack in France. Hearings were held to investigate charges that he had stolen supplies he was supposed to transport to French colonies, and that he hadn't paid taxes on all the loot he had won on the Nevis expedition. After more than twenty-five years of legal battles, his widow did have to pay back some of the money she'd inherited.

Iberville's actions weren't always honourable. A chance to make money often moved him to action as much as a desire to fight for his country, and he didn't always respect truces and terms of surrender. But whether his job was to take control of Hudson Bay, rediscover Louisiana, or harass the English whenever possible, he always got it done. He was a true knight, worthy of the title of chevalier, and of a place in history as New France's greatest soldier.

# Madeleine Jarret de Verchères

## 1678–1747

**M**ADELEINE JARRET grew up on a seigneury known as Verchères, near Montreal. A seigneury was a section of land granted by the king of France to a person who promised to clear and settle it. The person given the land was called a seigneur. Like the lords and knights given land in the Middle Ages, the seigneur usually acted as a landlord. He would let poor newcomers, known as habitants, build houses and start small farms on his land. In return, the habitants paid him a small amount of rent each year, often just some grain or a few chickens.

The first seigneurs in New France tended to be friends of the king back in France or people with connections to officials in Quebec. But in the late 1660s, Louis XIV tried to tempt soldiers to stay in the colony they'd been sent to protect by offering them seigneuries too. That's how Madeleine Jarret's father, François, got his land, which he named Verchères after a tiny village near where he was born in France. He and his wife, Marie Perrot, settled at Verchères on the St. Lawrence in 1672.

Madeleine Jarret came from a large family. She was the fourth of twelve children. Her father didn't have much money, so he kept on being a soldier as well as a part-time farmer. That meant he was often away from home. When he was gone, his wife took care of the children and managed his affairs.

Once, when Jarret was twelve and her father was away, Iroquois warriors attacked Verchères. At the time, the Iroquois were siding with the English against the French, so they often attacked the small forts on the seigneuries near Montreal. With her family safe inside the staked wooden walls, Jarret's mother managed to hold off the attackers for nearly two days until help arrived.

Two years later, on October 22, 1692, both of Madeleine's parents were away when the Iroquois attacked Verchères again. Historians don't know exactly what happened that day. Many think that over the years, the tale of fourteen-year-old Madeleine's heroic defence of Verchères was exaggerated quite a bit. It's hard for them to believe, for example, the story of how she was able to outrun an Iroquois warrior who got close enough to grab her neckerchief, yet couldn't catch her as she loosened it to escape. They also doubt claims that she dodged a flurry of shots from forty-five musket-firing Iroquois as she ran to safety.

Nevertheless, it does appear that Jarret acted bravely and quickly that morning when some Iroquois captured about twenty people working in the fields outside the fort. Somehow, she managed to make a dash for the fort, yelling for those inside to get their guns. Gasping for breath, she made it back to safety, only to find the few adults inside terrified. Jarret took charge. She put on a soldier's hat, grabbed a musket and raced to the top of the wall, calling for her two younger brothers and a couple of old men to do the same thing.

For hours, Jarret kept them firing their guns and making noises to give the impression that a lot of soldiers were defending the place. At one point, she also fired the cannon, scaring some of the warriors and warning other forts within earshot that danger was near. One version of what happened has her holding off her attackers like that for a week.

But once she had fired the cannon, people at other forts would have done the same thing, quickly passing the danger signal along the river to Montreal. It wouldn't have taken a week for reinforcements to get from there to Verchères, and it's not likely that the Iroquois would have stayed around for more than two or three days. They didn't want to get caught. Even so, Madeleine was able to control her own fear and keep a clear head for as long as it took to save her family and the fort. It's no wonder that the settlers thought she was a hero.

Unfortunately, Jarret's popularity faded somewhat after she left Verchères. She married a soldier named Pierre-Thomas Tarieu de La Pérade when she was twenty-eight, and went to live on his family's seigneury on the north shore of the St. Lawrence. But she and her husband treated their habitants badly. They often lost their tempers with them, and even beat them up. Some farmers took their wheat to other seigneurs' mills to have it ground into flour, and one even gave up his new lease when he found out that the La Pérades were going to be his landlords.

Sixty-nine-year-old Madame Madeleine La Pérade died during the first week of August in 1747. She was buried under her regular seat in the local parish church. Fourteen-year-old Mademoiselle Madeleine Jarret de Verchères lives on forever in history.

# James Wolfe
## 1727–1759

JAMES WOLFE was born in Westerham, England. He grew up and went to school there until he was ten, when his family moved to Greenwich, near London. Even when he was a little boy, he wanted to be a soldier, just like his dad. Whenever Colonel Edward Wolfe came home on leave, James and his younger brother, Ned, could hardly wait to hear his stories of adventure and bravery. James often asked his dad when he'd be old enough to go away with him.

In the summer of 1740, Colonel Wolfe finally agreed to let James join him as a volunteer. That way, he'd at least be able to keep an eye on his son while he got his first taste of military life. But a few months later, the colonel had to send the tall, skinny thirteen-year-old back home. James had been sick right from the start. Worst of all, he had learned that even the slightest bobbing of a ship sent him into spasms of seasickness.

Wolfe would suffer from poor health and be plagued by

seasickness for the rest of his life, but he was determined not to let anything stand in the way of his dream of a military career. In November 1741, after much pestering, his father got him an appointment as a junior officer in his regiment. Mercifully, Wolfe didn't get to join his father, who was serving thousands of kilometres from home at the time. The regiment had recently become a marine corps, and Wolfe might not have survived the long months at sea.

Instead, in March 1742, Wolfe was transferred to an infantry regiment and, at fifteen, began his life as a soldier. His first posting was in Belgium, where he spent what he saw as many boring months marching from town to town, practising drills, eating poor food and trying to sleep in crowded, smelly quarters. He was ready to fight. Instead, he trained all day and filled his free time reading, playing his flute and writing long letters home to his parents and friends.

In 1743, Wolfe finally got his wish. He and his brother, Ned, who had also joined the regiment by then, saw their first action in Germany in skirmishes against the French. That summer, Wolfe learned the importance of keeping one's position and holding off firing until the enemy was close enough to hit. It was a lesson he would never forget. The duke of Cumberland noticed how brave and disciplined he was during the fighting, and recommended that he be promoted to captain.

Young Captain Wolfe spent that Christmas back in Belgium, while Ned spent the holidays at home on sick leave. The next summer, Wolfe received the heartbreaking news that Ned had died of tuberculosis. Some historians say that details of Wolfe's many illnesses suggest he may have had TB too. Nevertheless, he continued to do his duty bravely and well. After seeing further action against the French in 1745, he was made a brigade-major.

A year later, British troops, Wolfe among them, were rushed

back to England to fight off attacking Scottish Highlanders, and in 1746 Wolfe fought at the famous Battle of Culloden in Scotland, when the English finally defeated the Highlanders. It was then that Wolfe showed how decent yet bold he could be. When his commander, a mean general with a nasty reputation, ordered him to shoot a Scot lying wounded on the battlefield, Wolfe refused, saying, "I cannot consent to be an executioner." It's said that this refusal inspired Highland regiment soldiers to serve proudly under Wolfe's command years later in Canada.

Over the next few years, Wolfe worked his way up the military ranks. In 1747, he was wounded in action and finally got to spend Christmas at home, recovering. In 1748, while enjoying another brief leave in London, he fell in love with a young woman named Elizabeth Lawson, but his mother didn't think she was the right girl for him. Arguments over whether he should keep seeing her led to a brief split from his family, adding to his loneliness when he was sent to Scotland as a major.

With the commander, Col. Edward Cornwallis, away in North America, Wolfe was left in charge of the 20th Foot Regiment and did an excellent job. Soldiers came to respect him as a fair leader who sincerely cared about them. He also led by example, avoiding the drunkenness and womanizing of which many other officers were so often guilty. In 1750, when he was appointed lieutenant-colonel at age twenty-three, he officially became the regiment's commander.

Struggling with several bouts of sickness that often left him too sore and weak to move, Wolfe still kept his troops in Scotland well trained, fit and disciplined. He himself tried to keep mentally fit, teaching himself academic subjects such as Latin and mathematics. During a six-month leave in Paris, he also became fairly fluent in French. He continued to write to Elizabeth Lawson, and to see her occasionally when he was back home. But because of his mother's ongoing opposition, the romance faded and Lawson eventually got tired of waiting for her first love to propose.

In May 1756, as part of a European conflict known as the Seven Years War, Britain officially declared war against France. William Pitt, the British prime minister at the time, had a plan to destroy France's naval power and take over all its colonies while the French and their allies were busy fighting in Europe. Wolfe's first action in this war was a disastrous British effort on the French coast in 1757. He was disgusted with his commander's actions, convinced that he didn't attack when he should have.

Soon after, Wolfe was appointed colonel of his own new regiment, and in early January 1758, he received orders to get to London as fast as he could because British forces had just been ordered to sail for North America. Wolfe was excited. At last, he would be able to command his own men and use all the military knowledge and skills he had learned over the years. But the tall, rail-thin young man was worried too. How would he ever survive so many days aboard ship, crossing the Atlantic?

Wolfe sailed from England in late February as a brigade commander in an expedition headed by Maj.-Gen. Jeffery Amherst. Amherst's orders were to attack and capture the French fortification of Louisbourg, on Île Royale (now Cape Breton Island). Wolfe arrived at Halifax, weak but eager, on May 9, and Amherst arrived about three weeks later. On June 8, Wolfe led a successful attack against Louisbourg, and after a six-week siege, the French governor surrendered. Amherst was very pleased with his young colonel's actions, and immediately sent word back to England of how well Wolfe had done.

Wolfe was all ready to keep going and attack Quebec next, but the navy's admiral didn't think that was a good idea. With cold weather on the way, there was a good chance ships would be trapped by ice in the St. Lawrence if the battle went on too long.

So Wolfe spent much of September attacking and destroying French settlements in the Gaspé area. When he arrived back in England in November, he received a hero's welcome.

In the next two months, the brave young bachelor was in great demand at all the best dinner parties. Although they were never officially engaged, he won the heart of, and a promise of marriage from, a wealthy young woman named Katherine Lowther. Again, his mother wasn't in favour of the match. She had wanted, as was the custom, to be the one to choose his wife. Still, when Wolfe sailed for Quebec in February 1759, he carried with him a small painting, or miniature, of his beloved Katherine. But he was never to see her again.

In January 1759, Wolfe was given the job of capturing Quebec. On April 30, he was back in Halifax, and by early June, he and a huge flotilla of ships under the British commander-in-chief, Sir Charles Saunders, were working their way up the St. Lawrence. On June 27, Wolfe landed most of his troops on Île d'Orléans, just east of Quebec.

The young general spent a frustrating July trying to figure out how best to attack Quebec. High above the St. Lawrence, the city proved to be a very difficult target. Even though the French, led by Gen. Louis-Joseph de Montcalm (see p. 118), had twice as many men as he did, Wolfe was sure his well-trained soldiers could beat them if he could only draw them out into battle.

At the beginning of July, Wolfe began bombarding the city with cannon fire from across the river. At the end of July, he had to call off an attack from the east after losing nearly two hundred men. In August, physically sick and frustrated, he ordered destructive attacks on villages along the river to the east. At times, he seemed unable to make up his mind about what to do next. But after some debate with his officers in early September, plans to end the siege with a sneak attack at night began to take shape.

Good timing, great soldiering and some luck all worked together for Wolfe in the early hours of September 13. At about 4 a.m., British troops landed just west of the city, headed straight up the cliffs and took battle positions on a field known as the Plains of Abraham. At about 10 a.m., Montcalm did what Wolfe had hoped he would do—he attacked. Led by Wolfe, the British held their position and didn't fire until their targets were within range. Then Wolfe began to move forward.

The first shot hit Wolfe in the hand, the next two in the torso. Soldiers rushed their young general's body from the battlefield, but it was too late. The last two shots had been fatal. The French general, Montcalm, was also fatally wounded that morning, and died the next day. The battle ended quickly, with the English taking Quebec and most of the French retreating across the St. Charles River.

The loss of Quebec marked the beginning of the end for the French. England went on to win the war, and Canada became British territory. But the British victory on the Plains of Abraham was bittersweet. England had lost a favourite son. Instead of welcoming home a conquering hero, the church bells of London rang out in mourning when the body of the valiant young general was brought home.

# Louis-Joseph de Montcalm

## 1712–1759

GENERATIONS OF Montcalm men made their way in the world as military leaders. That's what was expected of these aristocratic gentlemen. It was a family tradition to serve France like this. Bravery under fire and victory in battle brought new honour to the family name and often added to the family fortune.

However, the sons of noble families like the Montcalms didn't spend years living the grubby life of the lowest-ranked soldiers. It was customary for their parents to buy their first commissions as junior officers. That appears to be how Louis-Joseph de Montcalm became an ensign in the Regiment d'Hainault in 1721, when he was just eight, and a captain when he was seventeen.

But getting into the military this way didn't keep Montcalm from training, marching and fighting like everybody else. Family money could buy him a better horse and weapons, a warm overcoat, fitted boots and good food cooked by an aide, but it couldn't buy him safety. In fact, as an officer leading from the front, he was frequently in the line of fire.

In the 1730s and 1740s, France was often caught up in wars fought over who should take over when the kings of certain European countries died. Montcalm saw a lot of action during these conflicts. He was wounded during a French and Bavarian invasion of Austria, and again when France was fighting with its Spanish allies against Austria in Italy. He wasn't just badly wounded in Italy; his regiment was nearly wiped out and he was captured.

By then Montcalm was a colonel and had also been knighted by King Louis XV, so the Austrians saw him as both a valuable prisoner and one whose word, or parole, could be trusted. When he was well enough to travel, they let him return to Paris. Officially he was still a prisoner, and as long as he was on parole, he couldn't rejoin the fighting. In the spring of 1747, he was promoted to brigadier. Soon after, the French and Austrians agreed to exchange prisoners, Montcalm among them. As soon as he was officially released, he headed right back to Italy and was wounded a third time.

This time Montcalm made it home. He had married Angélique-Louise Talon de Boulay in 1736. After eleven campaigns, and with France at peace in 1748, he was finally able to settle down with her and their five children. He spent the next seven years with his family, enjoying life as a country gentleman and making a trip every now and then to inspect his regiment.

In 1754, fighting broke out between the French and British

over territory in the Ohio River Valley in North America. Tensions between France and England began to build in Europe too. It soon became clear that Montcalm's days of easy living were numbered. In 1756, with the start of the Seven Years War just two months away, he was made major-general in charge of forces in New France. A few weeks later, in early April, he was on his way to Canada with a convoy of ships and soldiers.

Montcalm had no experience planning full campaigns or being responsible for so many troops. But France's minister of war knew more experienced generals would be needed to beat England on the home front. Besides, Montcalm's orders made it clear that he would be in charge of the troops only once New France's governor-general, Pierre de Rigaud de Vaudreuil, had decided what they should do. In other words, Vaudreuil would be Montcalm's commander.

From the very beginning that arrangement caused problems. Both men were rather vain, and both liked to impress people with how wonderfully they did things. So when something went well, they fought over who should get the credit, and when something went badly, each one was quick to blame the other. Montcalm saw Vaudreuil as someone who couldn't make up his mind. Vaudreuil saw Montcalm as a snobbish outsider who didn't appreciate the courage and fighting ability of the colony's French-Canadian soldiers and Iroquois allies.

It was clear to both men that British and American forces could attack from three directions—down the Great Lakes to Montreal, down the Richelieu River from Lake George and Lake Champlain, and up the St. Lawrence from the Atlantic. In 1756, Louisbourg (on Cape Breton Island) was still in French hands, standing guard over the St. Lawrence, so Montcalm's first assignment was to join Vaudreuil's brother at Fort Frontenac (now Kingston) in late July and destroy Fort Oswego across Lake Ontario.

The attack on Oswego was a great victory for the French, and it won them much-needed British ships, supplies and weapons too. Vaudreuil was proud that his plan had worked so well, but Montcalm wasn't impressed. He didn't like the way the Canadians fought. He preferred the European siege-and-battles approach to warfare, and thought the quick raids and guerrilla warfare the Canadians favoured were dangerous and disgraceful. Even though the French now had control of Lake Ontario, neither man could resist criticizing the other.

In July 1757, Vaudreuil ordered Montcalm south with eight thousand troops to take and destroy Fort William Henry at the lower tip of Lake Champlain. Montcalm reached the fort on August 3, and after just six days, the twenty-five hundred British troops waved the white flag. Montcalm was very pleased with his victory, and rightly so. The British had suffered a major defeat. However, Vaudreuil was furious that Montcalm had not followed all his orders and gone on to destroy Fort Edward, just another day's march away.

By the winter, Montcalm was becoming more and more pessimistic about French chances of holding off the British. France seemed to be more interested in supporting its armies in Europe than in sending him the extra troops and supplies he kept asking for. As well, there were serious food shortages in Quebec, he was having to use more of his own money to live as a general should, and he suspected many Quebec officials were taking some of the money meant to run the colony. Still, he didn't turn down invitations to the expensive, fancy banquets he complained about, and he wasn't above wishing the ladies paid as much attention to him as they did to some of the taller, less portly generals.

By the summer of 1758, relations between Montcalm and Vaudreuil were worse than ever. Montcalm actually refused Vaudreuil's orders to take extra French-Canadian soldiers with him to Lake Champlain to stop thousands of British and Americans who were starting to move north. On July 8, the British attacked Montcalm at Fort Ticonderoga. But he didn't just hold them off; he beat them soundly and chased after them as they retreated. Then he wrote home to France bragging about how he had won this great victory without the help of local troops. Again, Vaudreuil was furious, and asked France to recall and replace Montcalm. What he didn't know was that Montcalm had asked to be replaced too.

But there would be no recall for Montcalm. Louisbourg fell that summer, and both Montcalm and Vaudreuil knew that the British would be back the next spring. Still, each man hoped that sailing a fleet up the powerful, tide-ruled St. Lawrence would prove to be too much of a challenge for their opponents. But it wasn't, and by early July Gen. James Wolfe's (see p. 112) troops had set up cannons across the river from Quebec and begun bombarding the well-fortified city.

On July 31, French troops beat back Wolfe when he tried to attack the city from the east. After that, Montcalm was certain Wolfe would try to strike there again. Vaudreuil, however, feared an attack from the west and wanted to place more reinforcements there. In the end, it didn't really matter too much where the reinforcements were. Montcalm had at least twice as many troops as Wolfe, and historians agree that all he had to do was hold off the British and wait them out. Many of Wolfe's soldiers were sick with dysentery, their supplies were running low, and if they didn't leave soon, they'd be sitting ducks trapped in the ice when winter set in.

Montcalm couldn't believe his ears when a lookout raced in on the morning of September 13 to report that Wolfe and more than four thousand troops were in place just outside the city on the Plains of Abraham. How had they scaled the cliffs, he wondered, and what should he do next? Stay put, historians would answer. But Montcalm panicked and, without checking with Vaudreuil, did exactly what Wolfe hoped he would do. He led French troops out of the city to face the British.

Within minutes, the French were beating a retreat back towards the city's gates. Riding bravely through the fray, Montcalm tried to rally his troops, but he couldn't stop them from turning. Caught up in the rush for the gates, he was struck by two bullets. Slumped in the saddle and bleeding from his wounds, he was rushed to a doctor, but to no avail. The surgeon did what he could for the general, but Montcalm died at five the next morning.

Perhaps Montcalm was somewhat comforted with news that Wolfe had been killed the day before, but probably not. Trained in the European way of fighting, he would have been prepared to surrender honourably to, or accept surrender from, such a worthy opponent. But that meeting was never meant to be.

Under cover of darkness, most of the French troops escaped from Quebec and headed for Montreal to regroup and set up better defences there. Weeks before, Montcalm had left directions on how a surrender should take place and what the terms of surrender should be. After he died, the white flag was raised over Quebec and his instructions were carried out. Vaudreuil would be forced to surrender the rest of the colony a year later, and Britain would take control of Canada.

Montcalm's body was buried on the grounds of an Ursuline convent in the city he had failed to keep out of British hands. When news of his death reached France, people there felt that they had lost a great military hero. People in Quebec weren't so sure that's what he had been. However, that he was a brave soldier no one ever doubted, not even Vaudreuil.

# John Graves Simcoe
## 1752–1806

**B**ORN IN Northamptonshire, England, John Graves Simcoe had lost all of his family by age fourteen. His father, Capt. John Simcoe, was a British naval commander who died of pneumonia aboard a ship sailing up the St. Lawrence to take part in the 1759 siege of Quebec. Two of his brothers had died as babies, and in 1764 his third brother, Percy, drowned. Two years later his mother died, leaving him in the care of his godfather, Adm. Sir Thomas Graves, a close friend of his father's. A few months later, Admiral Graves enrolled his godson at Eton College, one of the finest schools in England.

Simcoe had been a good student at grammar school. He was very athletic and popular with his classmates. He continued to do well during his three years at Eton, but after a further year of study at Oxford University, he went back home to Exeter to learn more about what interested him most—military science. With the help of a private tutor, he learned everything he could about how battles were fought and wars were won or lost. Family friends had promised to arrange for him to become an officer, and he wanted to be well prepared when he began following in his father's and godfather's footsteps.

Simcoe joined the infantry in 1770 and was stationed at Plymouth. Five years later, he was sent overseas for the first time. By then, Britain was fighting the Revolutionary War in the United States, and Admiral Graves was in charge of a fleet of ships being sent to America to take control of Boston harbour. Simcoe was part of that fleet, and he saw his first action at Boston. For the next four years, he fought bravely and well for king and country.

Simcoe was involved in the capture of Long Island and New York, and was part of the force that drove Gen. George Washington's troops back through New Jersey and across the Delaware River. After Washington recrossed the Delaware, Simcoe was seriously wounded at the bloody battle of Brandywine, near Philadelphia. When he recovered, he was given command of a company of soldiers known as the Queen's Rangers. Under his command, the Queen's Rangers became a force to be feared by the Americans. Simcoe was wounded two more times during the war and, in 1779, was captured and spent three months in a small prison cell. His wounds, recurring migraine headaches and overall poor health finally got the better of him, and he had to give up command of the Rangers.

In December 1781, with the Americans victorious in their revolution, Simcoe sailed back to England. He returned home as a lieutenant-colonel with a reputation as a brave, skilful, loyal commander. One person who was impressed with the returning hero was Admiral Graves's young niece, Elizabeth Gwillim. She and Simcoe got to know each other when he was spending time at his godfather's, recovering his health. They fell in love and were married in December 1782. Gwillim had inherited a lot of money when her father died, and some people said Simcoe married her for her money. But theirs was a love that would last a lifetime. They would have eleven children.

Simcoe settled into life as a married country gentleman, but he kept himself informed about military activities and about what was going on in Britain's colonies, especially Canada. He'd always felt a close connection to Canada because his father had died there. His wife felt linked to the place too. Her father had made it to Quebec and fought in the Battle of the Plains of Abraham. With the American colonies lost, Simcoe saw Canada as the ideal refuge for the Loyalists, Americans who had stayed faithful to Britain during the Revolutionary War. Many of them had been attacked, robbed and even killed during and after the war. He was pleased to learn that thousands of them were making their way to safety in Canada.

In 1790, the British Parliament was preparing to pass the Constitutional Act, dividing Canada into two new provinces, Upper and Lower Canada (present-day Ontario and Quebec). Each province would have its own lieutenant-governor and governing council; a governor-general would still be responsible for the entire Canadian colony. Simcoe let it be known that he wanted to be Upper Canada's new lieutenant-governor. Then he could encourage more sturdy Loyalists to settle there and help him build a strong British colony in North America. Canada's governor-general, Sir Guy Carleton, had somebody else in mind for the lieutenant-governor's job, but King George III chose Simcoe.

In September 1791, a month after the Constitutional Act was passed, Simcoe, his wife and their two youngest children sailed for Quebec. Winter was already closing in when they arrived, so they made arrangements to stay there until the spring thaw. They finally set out for Kingston the following June, and Simcoe was sworn in as the new lieutenant-governor on July 8. The people of Kingston had been looking forward to having Simcoe and his council members living there. They were expecting their town to become the new province's capital. So they were disappointed when Simcoe announced that he wasn't staying. He had decided to move to Newark (now Niagara-on-the-Lake).

When the Simcoes arrived at Newark at the end of July, they found that repairs to their place weren't done yet, so they moved into three large tents. When the weather turned cold, the sides of the tents were boarded up to keep out the snow. Simcoe spent the fall setting the wheels of government in motion. That winter he travelled west to what is now Brantford, on the Grand River, and was royally welcomed by Joseph Brant and his Six Nations people. (Brant was the Mohawk leader whose people had been loyal, hard-fighting allies of the British during the American Revolution.) Then Simcoe went on to Detroit, which was still in Canadian hands, and checked out its defences against a possible American attack. On that same trip he renamed the La Tranche River the Thames, and he chose a site on that river where he vowed to build a permanent capital called London.

When Simcoe got back to Newark, he was horrified to hear that a Queenston man had tied up his black servant girl, thrown her in a boat and taken her, kicking and screaming, across the river to the United States to sell her to an American. Legally, the man was within his rights, but Simcoe was furious that such a thing could happen in Upper Canada. He immediately drew up a new law that would end slavery in the province, but slaveholders said the law was unfair because it would take away their valuable property. Simcoe had to make changes to his proposed Slave Act so that provincial representatives would pass it. The new law didn't free people who were already slaves, but it did guarantee that from that year—1793—on, everyone born in or coming to Upper Canada would be free. It would take another forty years for Great Britain to ban slavery, and nearly thirty more for the United States to do so.

In May 1793, Simcoe visited Toronto for the first time, and really liked its location on Lake Ontario from a military point of view. Always the planner with an eye to the future, Simcoe renamed it York and decided it would be the perfect spot for a naval base and a new town. Simcoe had reorganized the Queen's Rangers in Upper Canada, and that spring he put those troops to work building a road from Burlington Bay all the way to the future site of London. Later, the road would link Burlington to York. In October, Simcoe explored the countryside north of York to Georgian Bay, naming Lake Simcoe along the way in honour of his father. Afterwards, he started work on a road running from York to Lake Simcoe. He named the road after a neighbour in England, War Secretary Sir George Yonge. That road, Yonge Street, would one day be the longest street in the world.

Simcoe brought his family to York in July and, despite the mosquitoes and mud, Mrs. Simcoe liked the location too. He would make it the capital a year later. However, the Simcoes again found themselves spending the winter in temporary quarters, this time large canvas houses. In March 1794, Simcoe had to rush off to the Detroit area because Americans were moving into what Canada considered Native territory, south of Lake Erie. With Britain and France at war again, both he and Governor Carleton were worried that the United States would support the French by keeping British troops busy defending the Canadian border. Tensions continued to build during the summer, and in September Simcoe sent his family from Newark to Quebec for the winter. He felt they would be safer there if the Americans attacked Upper Canada.

The Americans never did attack. A treaty (Jay's Treaty) between the United States and Britain in November 1794 settled disputes between the two countries, giving some British posts such as Detroit and others in the Ohio Valley to the Americans and allowing both countries to use the Mississippi River transportation route. Joseph Brant felt let down by Simcoe, thinking that he could have done more to protect the rights of Aboriginal people being driven out of the Ohio Valley. But Simcoe didn't have the power to make Britain include protection for Native peoples in the treaty.

Simcoe governed Upper Canada for another year and a half. He continued to grant land to people willing to clear and settle it. He set aside one part of the land in each county as Church of England property and kept another part as crown land. He built more roads, and new towns eventually sprang up along them. He tried unsuccessfully to get more money from Governor Carleton and Britain to strengthen the colony's defences, and he failed to get a tax passed that would help build new schools. All the while, he fought a continuous battle to stay healthy. In July 1796, suffering from migraines, gout and possibly malaria, he took a year's leave of absence and returned to England, leaving behind a strong, healthy and growing British province.

Simcoe never returned to Upper Canada. He was promoted to lieutenant-general in November 1796, and a month later accepted the post of governor of San Domingo (now Haiti). By July 1797, he was too sick to stay on there. He moved back to his home in England, and wasn't given any major command positions for the next ten years. Finally, in 1806, he received an appointment that pleased him greatly. He was named commander-in-chief of British forces in India.

Simcoe saw this appointment as a long-delayed recognition of his many years of service and expertise. But he never got to take up that important post. While preparing to move to India, he was asked to make a quick trip to Portugal to discuss that country's defence plans against a possible attack by Napoleon's French forces. On the way to Lisbon, he became very ill. He was brought back to England but died before he got home to his family. In death, he was honoured in a way he had never been when he was alive. Troops lined the route in solemn salute when the funeral carriage bearing his body travelled back to his country estate, and military and political leaders attended his funeral. Today, Ontarians continue to remember and honour his many accomplishments each year on the first Monday in August. In several cities in the province, the August civic holiday is known as Simcoe Day.

# Laura (Ingersoll) Secord
## 1775–1868

I N THE EARLY 1800s, most of Europe was caught up in what were known as the Napoleonic Wars. As France flexed its military muscles, Britain often stopped American ships to make sure they weren't doing anything that might help Napoleon. Sometimes they forced American sailors on those ships to join the British navy. Fed up, the newly independent United States finally declared war on Britain in June 1812.

But the Americans had no intention of going all the way to England to do battle. Instead, they planned on marching into Canada and taking over the British colony without much of a fight. However, British, Canadian and Native forces defending the colony gave the Americans a lot more trouble than they had expected. One Canadian who helped ruin their plans was Laura Secord, a former American living near Niagara Falls.

Secord was born in Barrington, Massachusetts, on September 13, 1775, the same year the American War of Independence began. She was the oldest child of Thomas Ingersoll and Elizabeth Dewey. Ingersoll was a soldier with the Massachusetts forces who fought the British during the revolution.

When Laura was just eight, her mother died, leaving her to spend most of her time caring for her three little sisters. After about a year, her dad married again, but his second wife also became sick, and died four years later. Within months of her death, Ingersoll married a third time. This marriage would add three more sisters and four brothers to the Ingersoll clan.

When Laura was eighteen, her father decided to go to Upper Canada (now Ontario), where the government was giving settlers free land. Ingersoll promised to settle a large section on the Thames River (now Ingersoll, Ontario), but that would take time and money. So he first moved his family to Queenston and began to run a tavern there.

Over time, the Ingersolls met many of their neighbours in the busy communities around Niagara Falls. One family, the Secords, had come to the area from the United States in 1778. Like so many others who moved north then, the Secords had chosen to remain loyal to Britain after the American Revolution. Sometime in the late 1790s, Laura Ingersoll met, fell in love with and married one of the Secord boys, James.

James owned a farm at nearby St. David's, and at first the couple went to live there. But James wanted to be a merchant, not a farmer, so early on the Secords moved back to Queenston. Unfortunately, James wasn't a very good businessman, and he ended up owing a lot of people money. In fact, the Secords would often find themselves in debt or just getting by for the rest of their lives.

By the time the United States declared war on Britain in 1812, the Secords had five children, four girls and a boy. When American forces began attacking forts and towns around Niagara,

James joined the local militia. During the Battle of Queenston Heights, he was one of many left bleeding on the battlefield. When Laura heard that he'd been shot, she rushed to him and managed to get help to bring him home, only to find the house a mess. It had been looted by American soldiers on the run. Still, Laura nursed her husband there until he was strong enough to be moved, and then she took him to an in-law's house in St. David's, where the girls were already staying.

The next June, the Secords were back in Queenston, but life wasn't any easier for Laura. James was still weak from his wounds, Americans had taken over nearby Fort George and fighting was still going on in the area. One day some American soldiers showed up at the door and ordered Laura to feed them. While they were eating she overheard their plans, and what she learned horrified her. A large American force of nearly five hundred was on its way to make a sneak attack on fifty British led by Lt. James Fitzgibbon. The attack was to take place June 23. It was already June 21. Fitzgibbon would have to be told.

Fitzgibbon had set up his headquarters near Beaver Dams (now Thorold, Ontario), about 20 kilometres away. James wasn't well enough to make it that far. It would be up to Laura to warn the troops. At dawn the next morning, she tiptoed into her older daughters' room and asked them to take care of the younger children. Saying she had to visit their sick uncle in St. David's, she kissed them goodbye and was gone.

Laura's brother-in-law *had* been ill, so she'd have a good excuse for walking along the road alone if an American patrol stopped her and asked what she was up to. But Laura was hoping he had recovered enough to ride on to Fitzgibbon with her news. When she arrived in St. David's, she found him still too sick to do that. She would have to keep walking.

Laura's niece offered to go with her, but after four hours

trudging along under a hot sun, the young woman nearly collapsed. Secord left her behind at a place called Shipman's Corners and went on alone, along more back roads, across farmers' fields and through swampy bush. The route she was taking would add at least another 10 kilometres to her journey, but she wanted to do everything she could to avoid being caught.

By sunset, she was exhausted. Her long skirt was damp and muddy, her arms and legs were scratched, and she'd lost her shoes. Still, she pushed on, over a log across a creek and up one last hill. Suddenly, Iroquois soldiers acting as lookouts for the British burst out of the darkness. They thought they had caught a spy. After a few very tense minutes, Secord managed to convince them to take her to Fitzgibbon.

At first, the lieutenant didn't know what to make of the bedraggled little woman standing before him. But when he saw how determined she had been to tell him about an attack that might come as early as the next morning, he wisely decided to act on her warning.

The American forces didn't reach Beaver Dams until June 24, but when they did, Caughnawagan and Mohawk warriors were waiting for them. Fitzgibbon had set a trap for them and, thanks to the Native soldiers, it worked. The Americans surrendered to Fitzgibbon later that day.

The Battle of Beaver Dams was a serious loss for the Americans and a major victory for Fitzgibbon. It earned him a promotion. But it took a very long time for Laura Secord to receive any recognition for her role in the victory. She and James had two more children after the war ended in 1814, and James eventually got a small pension because of his war injuries, but their money troubles continued. It wasn't until 1861, twenty years after James died, that Laura's efforts were rewarded.

In the fall of 1860, Queen Victoria's eldest son, Prince Edward, visited Niagara Falls. During a ceremony marking the battle of Queenston Heights, the prince was given a list of all the veterans who had fought bravely for the British during the War of 1812. Weeks before, Laura Secord had insisted that her name and war story be added to the list, and rightly so. She had acted at least as bravely as many of the soldiers, and in some cases even more so. Apparently, the prince noticed the name of the only woman "veteran," and when he returned to England, he sent her a gift of £100, a small fortune for the times. That money would make her last few years of life a little easier.

On October 17, 1868, at age ninety-three, Laura Secord died. After that, people began to see Secord for the hero she was. As her story spread, some details got a little fuzzy, and at least one book about the war added information that wasn't true. She didn't make her 30-kilometre walk with a cow, she didn't carry a milk-pail and she didn't travel all through the night. But the monument at Queenston Heights, unveiled by the Canadian government on July 5, 1911, honoured her heroism simply and clearly. The three thousand people gathered that day for the unveiling passed by and read these powerful words on the plaque: "To Laura Ingersoll Secord, who saved her husband's life in the battle of these heights October 13th, 1812, and who risked her own in conveying to Captain Fitzgibbon information by which he won the victory of Beaver Dams."

# Isaac Brock
## 1769–1812

**W**HEN ISAAC BROCK was a young army officer stationed in Barbados, a fellow soldier who was always looking for a fight challenged him to a duel. Brock had to accept the troublemaker's challenge. If he didn't, his men would think he was a coward. But his opponent had deadly aim. The man had fought a lot of duels and even hired himself out to take other men's places in some of them.

Brock was a brave man, willing to die for his country, but he didn't want to die like this. How much, he wondered, was his opponent willing to lose? Because Brock was the one being challenged, he could choose how far apart they would be when they fired their pistols, so he chose the width of a handkerchief. Now the odds of both men being killed were equal. No one could miss at such close range. Suddenly the challenger wasn't so brave. In fact, he backed down, and ended up leaving the regiment in disgrace. Brock, however, went on to become the most admired leader his soldiers had ever known.

Brock's ability to size up an opponent, figure out his weaknesses and use them to his advantage would show up again and again in his brilliant military career. So would his bravery in the face of danger and his willingness to take risks. There were a few hints early on of the man he would become. Born on the English Channel island of Guernsey, he was usually the first one into the chilly, choppy water when he went swimming with friends. He could also hold his own in a boxing match. But while he mastered the fighting skills expected of a young man aiming for a career in the military, he didn't live for fighting. He enjoyed dinner parties and dancing, and he loved reading epic poetry about the great heroes of ancient Greece and Rome. He also studied and became fluent in French.

Like many other teenaged boys from fairly well-off families, Brock joined the British army as a junior officer when he was just fifteen. Six years later, in 1791, he was off to the West Indies, until he was sent home two years later on sick leave. Back in England, he was given the job of attracting new army recruits. In 1795, his older brother loaned him enough money to become the major shareholder, so to speak, in the 49th Infantry Regiment, and by 1797 he was the lieutenant-colonel in command of it. He saw his first real action when the regiment was sent to fight in Holland in 1799, and he received a minor wound there.

In June 1802, after two years of fighting in the Napoleonic Wars against France, Brock and his regiment were sent to Canada to strengthen British defences there. The French had provided the Americans with supplies during their Revolutionary War against Britain thirty years earlier, and now the Americans were starting to return the favour to Napoleon. Military experts were afraid that if the Americans decided to cause the British even more problems, they might attack Canada while most of the troops were busy fighting in Europe. Lower Canada (Quebec) was fairly well defended along the St. Lawrence, but the border along the Great Lakes wasn't secure. Brock's job was to make sure the Americans met with some resistance if they tried to invade Canada there.

After spending the winter in Montreal, Brock and most of the 49th Regiment were sent to Fort York (now Toronto). During his three-year stay there, Brock became very familiar with the territory he might have to defend. But he wasn't thrilled about sitting around waiting for something to happen while the real action was going on in Europe, and he didn't like being stuck in a small, muddy backwoods settlement like York. Besides, many people in Upper Canada didn't seem to be too worried about an American invasion. Most of them were Loyalists who had come to Canada after the American Revolution, and they still had friends and relatives in the United States. Some of them thought becoming part of the United States was a good idea, and even a few of his soldiers tried to desert and live across the border. He wasn't sure how loyal Upper Canadians would be if an attack did come.

In 1805, Brock was made a colonel. After a brief leave back in England, he was temporarily put in charge of all the forces in Canada until a new commander-in-chief arrived in 1807. During that time, he had the walls around Quebec strengthened and added to the number of cannons overlooking the St. Lawrence River. He also began changing the marine section of the army from simply troop transporters to a well-trained, navy-like force, complete with heavily armed ships. Late in 1807, he was promoted to brigadier-general, and in the summer of 1810 he was given command of the British forces in Upper Canada.

The next year, with the added rank of major-general to his credit, Brock suddenly found himself doing double duty. When Upper Canada's lieutenant-governor, Francis Gore, went home on a leave of absence, Brock was given that job too. A few months later, he learned that there was a command available for him back in Europe, something he had wanted for many years. But by then, relations with the Americans were getting very tense, and he didn't think it would be right to leave just when his men and his country might need him most. So he stayed on, trying to pry more troops and supplies from the acting governor-general and commander-in-chief, George Prevost, in Quebec, and trying to convince the legislative assembly in Upper Canada that more had to be done to get ready for possible all-out war.

But Prevost didn't want to do anything that would upset the Americans, and some of the assembly members figured that there wasn't much point to investing a lot of men and resources in a military effort that was probably going to fail anyway. More than ever, Brock doubted the loyalty of many of the people he was getting ready to defend. With a shortage of troops and a lack of support from the general population, Brock knew that he needed help, and for that help he turned to Britain's Aboriginal allies. The Americans, relentlessly driving Native people from their lands northwest of New England, had become the sworn enemies of many bands. Brock sympathized with Native leaders who were demanding that they be left to live in peace on their own land, and he felt that the area known as the Michigan territory should be theirs. He thought they might be able to help each other.

In February 1812, Brock secretly sent a message to a Scotsman named Robert Dickson who lived with people of the Sioux nation in the American midwest and had in effect become a Sioux war chief. In a letter that he wasn't even sure would reach Dickson, Brock asked for support, especially in the area around Fort

Michilimackinac, a former French trading post. Also known as Mackinac, this American-held fort controlled entry into three of the Great Lakes: Huron, Superior and Michigan. Brock wanted it back in Canadian hands, and he wanted Native forces to help him when he made his move to take it.

Prevost had ordered Brock not to do anything until the Americans made their first move. For Brock, that move came when the United States declared war on Britain on June 18, 1812. Without waiting for Prevost's approval, he sent orders to Capt. Charles Roberts, commander of St. Joseph's Island near Mackinac, giving him the green light to attack the Americans there if he thought he could manage such an effort. Brock didn't know yet that Dickson had got his message and had 130 Native warriors waiting for orders from Roberts. Word about the declaration of war still hadn't reached the Americans at Mackinac, so when Roberts decided to attack them on July 17, their commander was taken completely by surprise and surrendered immediately, before any lives were lost.

The capture of Mackinac changed everything in Upper Canada. As word of the victory spread, more volunteers started joining the militia, and Six Nations Mohawks around Montreal and the Grand River started to look at Brock in a new light. The tall, strongly built man was more than just a polite, handsome administrator from England. He was smart, he was decisive and he was a victorious warrior. When Tecumseh, the great Shawnee war chief, heard about how Brock had beaten the Americans, he led hundreds of his warriors north to help him. When American forces led by Gen. William Hull crossed the Detroit River and invaded Canada on July 12, 1812, Tecumseh was standing by in the area, waiting for Brock to act.

When news of Hull's invasion reached Brock at York, he raced with troops to Fort Amherstburg, across the river from the

Americans' Fort Detroit. There, he met Tecumseh for the first time. Each man was greatly impressed with the leadership qualities of the other, and together they planned an attack on Detroit. Unsure of what to do after he landed in Canada, Hull and his hundreds of troops had retreated there without attacking Fort Amherstburg.

Though he was outnumbered nearly two to one, Brock attacked on August 16. Hull was petrified at the thought of Tecumseh's warriors overrunning Detroit and slaughtering everyone. He didn't know that the Shawnee war chief had given his word that his troops wouldn't harm any prisoners. Brock didn't help matters by sending Hull a demand for surrender, saying he couldn't guarantee how his Native troops would behave. Just as he had when challenged to the duel years earlier, Brock had figured out what his enemy's fears and weaknesses were, and he took advantage of them. After a brief battle, Hull surrendered and British forces took control of the fort, hundreds of prisoners and a small fortune in military weapons and supplies.

Brock was now the hero of the moment, and Canadians rallied around him. Even Prevost had only praise for the daring young general who hadn't followed orders. But Brock barely had time to catch his breath. Thousands of American forces were heading for the border along the Niagara River. Brock rushed back to Fort George, near Niagara Falls, and began organizing his troops in the area. Again, he was outnumbered, but he figured he was in a much better position than the Americans were. They would have to fight the powerful crosscurrent of the Niagara River, and he would be waiting for them on the other side.

When the attack finally began on October 13, 1812, Brock was catching a few hours sleep at Fort George. The instant he heard cannon fire, he leapt on his horse and galloped to Queenston, rallying soldiers along the way. Troops that included the men of his own 49th Regiment were already firing at the Americans crossing the river. But as Brock pushed his horse up the hill to give orders to the men with the cannon there, he was horrified to find the gun in enemy hands. Some American soldiers had made it along a trail through the bush, taken over the cannon and were getting ready to pound the British below with their own weapon.

Brock knew he had to take back the cannon. Always one who believed that he must never send his men where he wouldn't go himself, he rounded up some soldiers from the 49th and led the charge up the hill on foot. His tall, red-jacketed form was their beacon as they climbed after him. It was also the perfect target for an American sniper. Brock was felled with one shot to the heart and died almost instantly. Horrified, the troops hesitated, but not for long. Spurred on by their desire to avenge their courageous leader's death, they and many enraged Mohawk warriors regrouped and fearlessly charged again.

The charging troops won back the heights that day, and the American forces suffered a devastating defeat. But the loss of Brock had been a horrible price to pay. He was buried with full honours at Fort George, and even the Americans across the river joined in the cannon salute to mark a fallen hero. Then it was back to fighting. In 1813, the Americans did invade Canada and take control of the Great Lakes for a while. The War of 1812 didn't end until the fall of 1814, with both sides agreeing to go back to the way things were before it had started.

Today, Canada's tallest monument towers above the Niagara River at Queenston Heights, in clear view from each side of the Canadian–American border. It marks the final resting place of Brock's remains, and it honours him for saving Upper Canada in 1812.

# Alexander Mackenzie
## 1764–1820

ALEXANDER MACKENZIE knew what the rising water meant. The night before, when his men had noticed that the supplies were getting wet, he had said it was because of the wind. But there was no wind this time, and the water surrounding their island camp was getting higher again. There was only one logical explanation: tides. Mackenzie finally had to accept what he had suspected for days. He had gone the wrong way.

Mackenzie had set out from Fort Chipewyan on Lake Athabasca nearly six weeks earlier in search of a water route to the Pacific Ocean. Now he had to face the fact that he had reached the Arctic Ocean instead. His first attempt at exploration had failed. The truth hurt.

Mackenzie hadn't started out wanting to be a North American explorer. He was born at Stornoway, in the Scottish Outer Hebrides, and might never have left his island home if tragedy hadn't struck his family. When he was just ten, his mother died and his father took him across to New York City to stay with an uncle and two aunts. He hadn't been there long when the American Revolution began. His father and his uncle both joined a regiment loyal to Britain, and in 1778 his aunts sent him to live with family friends in Montreal, where it was safer.

Mackenzie went to school there until he was fifteen. Then he got a job keeping the records and accounts for Finlay, Gregory and Company, Montreal fur merchants. Over the next five years, he learned everything he could about the business, and decided that one could become very rich as a fur trader. In 1784, his firm sent him to an area around Detroit to experience life as a trader first-hand.

Mackenzie must have made some good deals for the company because the next year he was offered a share in its spin-off firm, Gregory MacLeod. In return he was expected to set up a small trading post in the Churchill River region of what's now Saskatchewan, where there was already fierce competition between traders from both the Hudson's Bay Company and the rival North West Company.

From 1785 to 1787, Mackenzie worked hard to attract hunters to his independent trading post. Instead of being driven out of business by a nearby Nor'Westers' post, he did so well that his firm was offered a partnership in the North West Company in 1787. That fall, he travelled farther west, to the Athabasca River, to spend the winter with another North West Company trader, Peter Pond.

Pond had been a trader for almost twenty-five years, and he had learned a lot about the geography of the northwest. He had listened carefully to what Native people living in the area told him about their travels, and he also studied reports about Capt. James Cook's voyage up the west coast in the late 1770s. All the information he had gathered left him convinced that there was a water link between Great Slave Lake and the Pacific Ocean.

Listening to Pond, Mackenzie began to think of how much cheaper it would be to ship furs from the northwest to Europe in bulk instead of paddling and portaging them thousands of kilometres back to Montreal. If Pond was right, the luxurious sea-otter pelts of the Pacific coast were only a tempting six-day journey west of Great Slave Lake.

In the spring of 1788, Pond quit the fur trade, leaving the Athabasca territory in Mackenzie's hands. The next year, Mackenzie sent his cousin, Roderick Mackenzie, north to build Fort Chipewyan at the southern tip of Lake Athabasca. It was to be the base camp from which Mackenzie would begin his search for a western water route to the sea.

Mackenzie set out from Fort Chipewyan on June 3, 1789. With him were four experienced voyageurs, the Native wives of two of the French Canadians, a German, a skilled Chipewyan trader named Matonabbee and his two wives, and two other Native men. After about two weeks fighting rapids and making portages, the three canoes reached Great Slave Lake. There was still some ice on the lake, but it was warm enough to bring out choking clouds of blackflies and mosquitoes searching for blood.

With the help of a local Yellowknife Native guide, Mackenzie made it out of the lake onto a major river flowing west. Excited, he pushed himself and his team to cover nearly 130 kilometres a day. But after a week or so, his excitement began to fade. The huge river seemed to be flowing more north than west with each passing day. On July 13, 1789, when he camped on what is now Garry Island at the mouth of the river that bears his name, he finally admitted he had reached the wrong ocean. Then, when he saw the vast, frozen Arctic stretching before him, he also realized there was no usable shipping passage across the top of the continent either. On July 16, he started the long upstream journey back to Fort Chipewyan.

Mackenzie now knew that Pond had been wrong about two things: the Pacific was a lot more than six days away, and the rivers flowing out of Great Slave Lake drained into the Arctic. In 1792, armed with that information and better navigational equipment, he set out again from Fort Chipewyan. This time he headed up the Peace River and built Fort Fork near what's now Peace River, Alberta.

Mackenzie spent the winter there, and on May 9, 1793, he and nine other men began an incredible journey westward across the Rockies. They paddled, portaged, climbed and scrambled along the Peace River, up the Parsnip, and down the Fraser. At one point, Natives warned them that going any farther down the Fraser meant certain death, so Mackenzie backtracked up the Fraser to the West Road River and, finally, down the Bella Coola. On July 21, their clothes torn and their patched canoe barely held together with tree gum, Mackenzie's exhausted band of men caught their first sight of the great western sea. It was the right ocean this time.

By August 24, Mackenzie and his companions were safely back at Fort Chipewyan. That winter he tried to complete the detailed journals he had kept along the way, but he found he couldn't concentrate on them. As the days passed, he thought more and more about going back to Montreal. He did so in the spring of 1794, never to go exploring again.

Mackenzie spent the next five years trying unsuccessfully to reorganize the entire Canadian fur-trading business. In November 1799, he sailed to England. He published his journals two years later, and they soon became best-sellers. In 1802 he was knighted by King George III, and in 1804 he was back in Canada serving as an elected member in the Assembly of Lower Canada (now Quebec). But he soon found politics boring and returned to London.

In 1812, Mackenzie married fourteen-year-old Geddes Mackenzie and settled at her family's estate in Scotland. The couple had three children and lived the comfortable life of the upper class. The first European, and most likely the first person, ever to cross North America north of Mexico attended balls and dinner parties with his wife in London in the spring, and spent the rest of the year enjoying the peaceful Scottish countryside.

Mackenzie died in Scotland in March 1820. Back in Canada, on a large, flat rock face overlooking the Pacific, some words he had printed in red dye seventeen years earlier were still clearly visible. They marked his passing as no tombstone could: "Alex Mackenzie, from Canada, by land, 22d July 1793."

# Thomas Douglas
# (Lord Selkirk)
## 1771–1820

THOMAS DOUGLAS was born on St. Mary's Isle, on the south coast of Scotland. His father was Dunbar Hamilton Douglas, the fourth earl of Selkirk. Lord Selkirk was a wealthy man who owned a lot of land in Scotland and Saint John's Island (now Prince Edward Island). When Thomas was fourteen, he began attending the University of Edinburgh. He studied arts-related subjects, plus a few courses in law, and proved to be quite a good writer. Fellow students found him to be a friendly, unselfish, quiet young man.

When Douglas graduated in 1792, he spent some time travelling around the Scottish Highlands, and was impressed by the hard-working, rugged Scots he met there. But the poverty he saw worried him. Many tenant farmers were being driven off land they had lived on for generations to make way for large-scale sheep farming. Something similar was happening in Ireland and other parts of Britain and Europe. Many poor people were moving to cities to work in the new factories sprouting up everywhere, but they often ended up paying very high rents to live in dirty, crowded housing. Douglas thought they'd be better off farming, and he wished he could help them get back to the land. But any ideas he came up with would cost more money than he had.

As Lord Selkirk's son, Douglas enjoyed a very comfortable lifestyle, but he never expected to get much of his family's wealth. Traditionally, property and titles were passed down to the oldest son, and Douglas was the youngest of seven boys. Two of his brothers had died when they were little, but he still had four older brothers. However, tragedy struck five times in the next few years. After he returned from university, two of his brothers died of tuberculosis, the other two died of yellow fever, and in 1799 his father died. Suddenly, at twenty-eight, Douglas had become the fifth earl of Selkirk, and everyone was calling him lord.

Selkirk now had the money to put his ideas into action. Many people in Ireland had rebelled because they were near starvation, so he decided to try to help them first. He believed they would make great settlers in British North America (Canada), and he wanted to help them get there. But the British government thought that was a bad idea, and wouldn't grant him any land in Upper Canada. So in 1803, he paid for a group of Scottish Highlanders to sail to Saint John's Island and settle on land he'd inherited from his father. The new families loved it there and were soon busy building houses and planting crops.

In 1804, Selkirk decided to visit Canada. He asked everybody he met about life there, and took notes on what he heard and saw. He also learned a lot about the fur-trading business and scouted out possible sites for new settlements. Canada's lieutenant-governor liked Selkirk's idea of bringing more British settlers to live near the American border, and he granted him a large section of land on the northeast end of Lake St. Clair, near the Detroit River. Selkirk called the place Baldoon and gave a man named William Burn the job of getting the place ready for settlers. Unfortunately, the land was swampy, Burn got lonely and drank too much, the few Highlanders who arrived got sick, and crops failed, so hardly anyone stayed on to farm for very long.

Back in Scotland, Selkirk didn't let the failure at Baldoon stop him from coming up with new settlement plans, but the British government wasn't interested in any of them. Fortunately, his marriage to twenty-one-year-old Jean Wedderburn in 1807 brought him not only new-found happiness, but also another chance to make his settlement dreams come true. Over the next few years, Wedderburn's brother and Selkirk bought enough shares in the Hudson's Bay Company (HBC) to have a say in the fur-trading company's decisions. That's how, in 1811, he got the company's directors to give him a huge grant of land around the Red and Assiniboine rivers (now southern Manitoba, and northern Minnesota and North Dakota).

Selkirk was sure Scottish families could make a go of it there, and if they happened to take some of the fur-trade business away from the North West Company (NWC) operating in the area, so much the better. For once, he might not lose money helping others get a new start. But people working for the NWC, especially Métis hunters and traders, didn't like the idea at all. Settlers would clear land and drive off the fur-bearing animals and the buffalo herds on which they depended for food. Even many HBC traders saw the proposed settlement as a threat, but they weren't major shareholders the way Selkirk was, and their opinions didn't count for much.

So there was strong opposition to the Red River settlement right from the start, and like Selkirk's other schemes, it ran into all sorts of practical difficulties too. Selkirk chose a man named Miles MacDonell to be governor of Assiniboia, the name of the new territory. MacDonell and the first group of Highlanders arrived at York Factory on Hudson Bay in the fall of 1811, but by then it was too late to travel south, so they had to spend the winter there. When the ice finally melted the following June, they set off in flat-bottomed boats they had built and worked their way down rivers and lakes until they reached the Red River late in August 1812. Some of the men started building Fort Douglas, named after their patron, but MacDonell sent the rest south to Pembina because there wasn't enough food to last the winter.

It wasn't until May 1813 that the settlers came back and started planting crops. But with only hoes to prepare the ground, they found the work exhausting. Worse still, the crops failed and most of the people had to spend another winter at Pembina. The next year, to help the colony survive, MacDonell gave an order saying no supplies could leave Assiniboia without a special licence from him. This infuriated both the Métis who sold dried buffalo meat, or pemmican, to fur traders and the NWC traders who took it with them on their travels.

Angry Nor'Westers began harassing the settlers and even talked some of them into moving east to Upper Canada. Eventually they captured Fort Douglas, arrested MacDonell and sent him to Montreal to be tried for confiscating their supplies. Selkirk sailed to Canada in 1815, intending to visit the troubled colony himself, but that fall he learned that most of it had been burned. He went to Montreal to confront NWC officials about what had happened, but they figured he was more interested in

HBC profits than in the welfare of his settlers and ignored his protests.

Just as he was about to leave for Red River in the spring of 1816, Selkirk learned that some of the settlers had returned there and were trying to farm again. He had a merchant named Robert Semple appointed as the new governor, and started making arrangements to go there himself with troops, supplies and weapons. But in July 1816, news reached him at Sault Ste. Marie that Semple and twenty or so settlers had been killed at Seven Oaks (now Winnipeg) when they got into a fight with some angry Nor'Westers. Enraged, Selkirk headed straight to Fort William, arrested some NWC officials he found there and sent them east under guard to stand trial for murder. Then he went on to Red River, took back Fort Douglas, made peace with local Native people, bought some land from them and started rebuilding his dream colony.

However, trouble was brewing back in Montreal. The NWC said that Selkirk had illegally taken Fort William and confiscated the furs there, and that he had to return to the east to stand trial on these charges. He went back via the United States because he felt his life was in danger. He spent the next year or so trying to clear his name and to have those responsible for the deaths of Semple and the other settlers brought to justice. But most of them jumped bail. Just when it looked as if he was going to be found not guilty in his own trial, the judge adjourned the case without letting the jury reach a verdict.

Sick, exhausted and fed up with the legal system in Canada, Selkirk sailed for London in 1818. He was determined to tell colonial officials there what had really happened in Canada and to clear his name. But tuberculosis was sapping his strength, and he had little energy left to fight for himself or his settlement. His wife, who had stayed in Montreal to take care of his financial affairs, sailed home in 1819 and took him to the south of France for the winter.

The next spring, merger talks began between the HBC and the NWC, and Selkirk was offered a lot of money for his HBC shares. Even though he was very sick and deeply in debt, however, he refused to sell them because the HBC wouldn't promise to take care of his Red River settlers. He died shortly afterwards, on April 8, 1820. People who questioned his motives for getting the Red River land grant had often called him the trader lord, but to the end he remained deeply concerned about the people he had brought to Canada to have a better life.

# Shawnadithit
## 1801?–1829

S HAWNADITHIT was a Beothuk. The Beothuk were a group of Aboriginal people who lived in Newfoundland for at least a thousand years, until the early 1800s. One day in March 1819, when she was about eighteen years old, Shawnadithit ran from her *mamateek* (a wigwam-like house) and took shelter in the woods. From the safety of her hiding place, she watched as her aunt Demasduwit stumbled through the snow, trying to get away from a small group of white men led by a man called John Peyton. They had come to get back supplies and equipment the Beothuks had stolen from them. Shawnadithit watched her aunt being captured. She also saw her uncle die.

When Demasduwit was being led away, her husband, Nonosbawsut, had followed at a distance, trying to figure out how to rescue her. Suddenly, he had stepped out of the woods and confronted Peyton, hoping to convince him to let her go. But the men hadn't understood what he was saying, and he hadn't understood them. They had thought he was about to attack them, and in the confusion that followed as his wife struggled to break free, he was shot and killed. When it was safe to do so, Shawnadithit's people carried Nonosbawsut's body back to a traditional burial ground and laid him to rest according to their customs. A year later, they would place Demasduwit's body beside his.

Shawnadithit hid in the woods again when other white men returned in 1820. She didn't know that they had come in peace. She had seen the group's leader nine years earlier, when she was just a young girl, and her memories of that encounter weren't pleasant. But all he and his men did this time was place Demasduwit's remains in one of the *mamateeks,* along with several gifts. Then, after looking around for a while, they left as quietly and respectfully as they had come.

The group's leader was a marine lieutenant named David Buchan. He had hoped that returning Demasduwit's body to her people would show them that he wanted to meet them, not hurt them. He had set out on a similar peace mission back in 1811, but it had ended in tragedy. For more than two hundred years, the Beothuks had been fighting with Europeans and falling victim to the new diseases they brought with them. Not surprisingly, then, the people Buchan met at Red Indian Lake in 1811 hadn't trusted him. He tried to show them that he had come in friendship, but he couldn't make himself understood. As a sign of good faith, he left two sailors with them while he went back along the trail to get some presents he had stored with his supplies. When he returned with the gifts, the Beothuks were nowhere to be seen and the two marines were dead, their heads mounted on poles in front of the *mamateeks.*

Buchan wasn't the first to try to reach out to the Red Indians, the name Europeans gave the Beothuks because they painted their bodies with a rust-coloured iron oxide clay called ochre. In 1768, a British navy captain named John Cartwright set out on an expedition to try to meet with some Beothuk people, but he found none. Of the thousand or so living in Newfoundland before Europeans started coming there to fish, there were only two to three hundred left. Many had died fighting with Mi'kmaq hunters who paddled over from Labrador every now and then. Others were killed carrying out hit-and-run raids to steal iron tools and supplies from European newcomers. A few were simply shot on sight by frightened or murderous settlers, and several died of smallpox or measles.

When Demasduwit was captured, she was left with a family named Leigh in Twillingate. The Leighs cared for her during the winter and taught her some English. In the spring, she was taken by boat to St. John's, but she didn't want to stay there. She missed being with her people. Unfortunately, several tries to find some Beothuks and return her to them failed. Later that fall, she died of tuberculosis. But Shawnadithit didn't know that was how her aunt had died. All she knew was that her band of Beothuks was getting smaller and smaller, and it was becoming very difficult for its members to find enough food to live. There weren't enough of them to carry out the fall caribou hunts any more, and white people were living all along the coast, where they used to travel to fish and hunt seals.

In early 1823, Shawnadithit's father fell through the ice and drowned. A trapper found her, her mother and her sister on the verge of starvation. He brought them to John Peyton at a place called Exploits. Peyton cared for them until the ice melted, then sailed with them to St. John's. As soon as they were well enough to travel, David Buchan, the British colony's acting governor at the time, made arrangements to return them to their people. They were given gifts, supplies and a small boat and left at a stream they knew well. Some weeks later, they were found again, hungry and desperate. They hadn't been able to find a single other Beothuk.

Shawnadithit's mother and sister were very ill, and died soon after they were found. Shawnadithit was returned to Peyton's home at Exploits, where she recovered and stayed for the next five years. She got along well with Peyton's family, and was especially good with the children. She learned English and showed a real talent for drawing. Every now and then she would spend some time alone in the woods, remembering her family and talking to them as if they were there with her.

In 1827, a merchant named William Epps Cormack set up the Beothuk Institute. Saddened by the knowledge that Shawnadithit might be the last of her people, he wanted to do what he could to preserve a record of their history, language and customs. In the fall of 1828, he brought Shawnadithit to stay with him at St. John's and wrote down everything she told him about the Beothuks. Shawnadithit also drew many pictures to show him how her people had done things like make a *mamateek* or a sea-going canoe out of birchbark, and how they had hunted seals and trapped caribou.

When Cormack left Newfoundland late in the winter of 1829, Attorney-General James Simms welcomed Shawnadithit into his home, but the tall, quiet, proud woman wasn't well. A doctor visited her often, trying to help her fight off the tuberculosis that had slowly been robbing her of her health. But on June 6, 1829, the white man's disease claimed its last known Beothuk victim. Her death marked the passing of her people from their island home. Her life gave voice to their story.

# George Vancouver
## 1757–1798

I F IT HADN'T been for Capt. George Vancouver, Canada's
motto might not be *A mare usque ad mare* (Latin for "From
sea to sea"). For nearly two hundred years, Spain had claimed
the entire Pacific coast of North America. By the 1770s, Spanish
explorers were landing at sites as far north as what's now Juneau,
Alaska, to make sure other countries knew they were serious
about their claim. Russian fur traders were also working their way
south along the west coast from Alaska.

When the Spanish king's representative in Mexico learned
that the Russians wanted to start a settlement on Nootka Sound
(on Vancouver Island), he sent an explorer named Esteban
Martinez there in 1787 to beat them to it. He wanted to make sure
the Russians stayed far north of the Spanish territory already

settled in California. When Martinez arrived at Nootka Sound, he did find British traders already doing business there, but he told them they were on Spanish territory, took over two of their ships and made them leave.

That action nearly started a war between Britain and Spain. But in 1790, the two countries worked out a deal known as the Nootka Convention. It included an agreement from the Spanish to give the Nootka Sound settlement back to the British. A new naval captain, George Vancouver, was given the job of officially accepting the settlement back from the Spanish. Vancouver had actually stayed at Nootka Sound for a few weeks in 1778, when he was still a young officer-in-training sailing with one of the world's greatest navigators, Capt. James Cook.

Vancouver, who was born near London, England, had joined the British Royal Navy when he was just fourteen. A year later, Cook had chosen him to be part of his crew on his second voyage in search of the so-called Great Southern Continent in Antarctic waters. During that three-year journey to parts unknown, Vancouver was with Cook when he sailed closer to the South Pole than anyone had recorded doing before. He saw the endless mountains of ice that stopped Cook from going any farther south. He also stared with Cook in awe at the large, mysterious stone figures standing guard over Easter Island when Cook became the first European to go there.

Time and again on that voyage, Vancouver was an eyewitness to history in the making. He was also very fortunate to work for, and learn from, Cook's brilliant astronomer, a man named William Wales. From Wales and Cook he learned the navigational and surveying skills that would one day earn him the captaincy of his own ship. Cook was very impressed with how competent and smart Vancouver was, and he chose him to be part of his third voyage in search of a Pacific coast entrance to the northwest passage across the top of Canada.

That's how Vancouver ended up at Nootka Sound at the end of March 1778. On the way north, Cook stopped there for a month to fix his ships and get fresh water and food. Because of that stopover, Vancouver became one of the first Europeans to set foot on what's now the British Columbia coast. After a few more months of exploring, Cook turned around and headed back down to the Sandwich Islands (Hawaii), which he had come across and named earlier on his way north. Cook had been warmly welcomed by the people there, and he thought he'd be able to trade with them for more supplies. But for some reason, the island residents weren't so happy to see him this time. On February 13, 1779, when Vancouver was on shore, he was stoned and beaten up, and barely escaped with his life. The next day, Cook was stabbed and beaten to death. Vancouver felt as if he had lost a father.

Cook's ships made it back to England by October 1780. That same month, Vancouver passed his lieutenant's exams. For the next nine years, he served on armed ships operating mainly in the Caribbean. During that time, the navy put his surveying skills to good use. While stationed in Jamaica, he made thousands of accurate depth measurements and carefully charted Kingston's impressive harbour. His tour of duty there ended in 1789, and he returned to England with a promotion to first lieutenant under his belt.

In 1790, Vancouver was serving on a ship patrolling the English Channel when he was ordered to go to London. There he received wonderful news. He was given command of the *Discovery,* Captain Cook's old ship. It and a smaller ship, the *Chatham,* under Capt. William Broughton, were to sail to the northwest coast of North America to accept the Nootka Sound settlement from the Spanish. Vancouver was put in charge of the expedition, which was to survey the Pacific coast, keeping an eye out for new settlement sites and rivers that ships could navigate to reach the interior. He was also to support the work of a botanist and astronomer sailing with him to collect valuable scientific information.

For Vancouver, it was a dream come true. He planned his course carefully, following Cook's route around southern Africa's Cape of Good Hope to the Pacific. He also followed Cook's example when it came to paying careful attention to having supplies of food that would keep his men from getting scurvy. On January 7, 1791, he proudly sailed the *Discovery* down the Thames River. The *Chatham* joined him at Falmouth at the end of March, and on April 1 he left on what would become one of the longest voyages ever made.

Throughout most of 1791, Vancouver sailed the South Pacific, surveying parts of the coastlines of New Zealand, Australia, Tasmania, Tahiti and Hawaii along the way. After spending the winter in the Hawaiian Islands, he continued northeast. The watch's call of "Land ho!" on April 17, 1792, marked his arrival on the North American coast, just north of San Francisco. Then the real work began. His instructions were to survey the coastline between the thirtieth parallel, or line of latitude, and 60° north, or all the way from California to Alaska! Cook had made a general outline on his voyage, but now the British wanted details— islands, straits, harbours, bays, inlets, sounds, navigable rivers emptying into the Pacific and locations of existing settlements. It was a huge task that would take three summers to do. He spent the winters in warmer southern climates.

Vancouver explored the Strait of Juan de Fuca, delighted in the beauty of Puget Sound, sailed right around Vancouver Island, mapped and named Burrard Inlet, ran aground near Queen Charlotte Sound, charted Prince William Sound and checked out

Cook Inlet. He was annoyed that he missed the mouth of the Columbia River on his first trip north, and if he had known, he would have been sorry to miss meeting Alexander Mackenzie (see p. 143). Vancouver was in the area when Mackenzie completed his historic cross-Canada journey to the Pacific in July 1793, but he didn't explore the Fraser River. He could tell from the path it cut through the awesome Rockies that ships couldn't sail up it from the sea. If he'd stayed around for another for two weeks, he might have met Mackenzie.

In 1792, Vancouver did meet the Spanish explorer Juan Francisco de la Bodega y Quadra, who was waiting for him at Nootka Sound. Quadra greeted Vancouver with a multi-course dinner served on silver dishes, and introduced him to another important dinner guest, the Nuu-Chah-Nulth (Nootka) chief, Maquinna. Quadra and Vancouver got along well right from the start, but Quadra was in no rush to have the Spanish settlement become a British port. For six weeks, he tried to talk Vancouver into changing the terms of the Nootka Sound agreement, but Vancouver said he had no authority to do so. Spain and England would eventually agree to share the port in 1794, but Vancouver's unwillingness to do so earlier, together with all the territorial claims he made for Britain as he surveyed the coast, went a long way towards ensuring that the area would one day become part of Canada, and not of Spain, Russia or the United States.

Vancouver finally returned home in October 1795. The maps and charts he had made proved to be invaluable. He had named and claimed hundreds of places not on earlier maps. He had also shown that there was no point looking any longer for an easy-to-sail northwest passage. He had made peace with the Hawaiians, and had even worked out an agreement with them to become part of Britain. For these and many other accomplishments, he should have been welcomed like a hero. But soon after his return, one of his junior officers, who was related to some very important people, including the prime minister, claimed that Vancouver had whipped him on the voyage, something captains were never supposed to do. Only ordinary sailors got punished with the lash.

The young man had behaved very badly at sea, but Vancouver hadn't ordered him lashed. No other sailor or officer backed up the whipping claim. Still, Vancouver had to fight to defend his good name, and that hurt. He had always taken such pride in his captaincy. He did occasionally lose his temper, but there's evidence that he did this because he was suffering from a disease that affected his thyroid gland and produced too many hormones. Besides, he clearly cared very much about the health and well-being of his men. In nearly five years at sea, he lost only one sailor to sickness.

Unfortunately, Vancouver himself had been getting sicker on the return voyage, and being back home didn't help. He moved to a little village near London to finish getting his journals, charts and maps into book form, but on May 12, 1798, he died and was buried in a simple ceremony in the local churchyard. His brother finished his book, *The Voyage of Discovery to the North Pacific Ocean and Round the World*. Only after it was published did people begin to realize what a great explorer, navigator and surveyor Vancouver had been.

# William Lyon Mackenzie
## 1795–1861

IN EARLY 1831, William Lyon Mackenzie was on his way to Quebec City when his ship got trapped in ice clogging the St. Lawrence River. Mackenzie wouldn't leave the damaged boat until he'd collected all his luggage. Then he staggered along with the other passengers who were carefully picking their way to the far-off shore. Suddenly, a huge crack appeared in the ice right in front of a woman near him. Without a second's thought for his own safety, Mackenzie dropped his luggage and threw himself across the gap, forming a human bridge over the frigid water.

The woman probably could have made it to shore some other way, but what Mackenzie did was typical of the man who would become a hero to many in Upper Canada (Ontario). He often acted impulsively, and rarely worried about the price he might have to pay for his actions. Sometimes, he even behaved foolishly or recklessly, but not even the threat of danger could stop him from doing what he thought was right.

Mackenzie was born at Dundee, Scotland, the only child of Daniel Mackenzie and Elizabeth Chalmers. His mother was eighteen years older than his father, and he was left fatherless when he was just three weeks old. His mother, a very religious woman, was a strict parent, but that didn't stop young Mackenzie from getting into mischief at school. He mimicked his teachers, made faces behind their backs and drew silly pictures on the board. When he was ten, he talked a few buddies into running away from home. They camped out in an old castle for several days before thoughts of home-cooked food and a warm bed got the better of them.

Mackenzie was an excellent student, and often helped classmates with their work. He was also a voracious reader. He made detailed notes on the nearly one thousand books he had devoured by the time he was a young man. Later, when he became a newspaper editor, he would mine those notes for article ideas and quotes. However, his first job was as an office clerk for a large wholesaler. When he turned nineteen, he borrowed enough money to open his own general store. He also ran a small library out of the shop. But times were tough, and after three years, the business failed. Discouraged, Mackenzie went to England and took whatever work he could find, but he wasted his money partying, drinking and gambling. He also became a single father and left his infant son in his mother's care.

In 1821, Mackenzie decided to shape up and start a new life in Canada. He sailed for Quebec in the spring. After a brief stint as an accountant in Montreal, he moved to York (now Toronto), where he and a friend opened a shop selling medicines and books. In 1822, he moved 80 kilometres southwest to Dundas and opened a general store. That same year, he sent for his mother, his young son and a woman named Isabel Baxter, whom he'd gone to school with in Scotland. Baxter had agreed to become his wife. Mackenzie met them in Quebec, and three weeks later he and Baxter were married. They would have thirteen children, six of whom died in childhood.

The store in Dundas did well, but Mackenzie needed something more in his life. He had an irresistible desire to share his opinions with others and to get them worked up about the same things that upset him. What bothered him most was the way Upper Canada was being governed. He believed that honesty and a willingness to do what the people needed and wanted were the keys to good government. He thought that officials weren't being honest about how they spent government money, and that they listened only to their friends, a group of powerful people nicknamed the Family Compact.

The Constitutional Act of 1791 had divided the British North American colony of Canada into two provinces, Upper and Lower Canada. Each province had an elected assembly that was supposed to act as the voice of the people who had elected it, but its decisions had to be approved by an executive council that could also pass laws. Council members were chosen by a British-appointed lieutenant-governor, who served as the head of government. He also appointed people to many government jobs and decided who got land grants. To poorer farmers and workers, the people running everything looked liked a powerful family that had made a deal, or compact, to make sure only their relatives got the well-paid government jobs and the best land to develop.

Mackenzie decided to fight the Family Compact with the most powerful weapon he knew—words. In the spring of 1824, he moved to Queenston, near Niagara Falls, and opened a newspaper called the *Colonial Advocate*. Six months later he moved the paper and his family to York. From the very first issue of the

*Colonial Advocate,* he was branded a troublemaker. The main reason the province's rulers were so upset with him was that he exposed what they were doing. He printed lists of everyone on the government payroll and how much they were making. He pointed out how they were all related or connected through business. He reported on land grants made to people with friends in high places. He wrote about how democratic the United States had become after the American Revolution, and about the many reforms taking place in Britain itself. Why, he asked, shouldn't people in Canada have similar reforms?

In June 1826, a bunch of rich young thugs decided to silence Mackenzie. They wrecked his house, where the paper's office was, broke his printing press and threw all the tiny letters, or type, into Lake Ontario. Nearby officials did nothing to stop the attack. The thugs were the sons of some very powerful families. Mackenzie was furious, and determined to get justice. He sued his attackers for damages, and got enough money to pay off some of his debts, buy new equipment and start the paper again.

News of the attack and the trial brought Mackenzie new readers and followers. With support growing weekly, Mackenzie decided to try to get elected to the assembly. In the 1827 election, he ran as a Reformer, the name given to the group opposed to the Family Compact's Conservatives, or Tories. He won in the county of York, and the Reformers won a huge majority. In the assembly, he complained louder than ever about government abuses, but the appointed council refused to approve some of the changes passed by the Reform majority in the assembly.

Mackenzie was re-elected in 1830, but a lot of other Reformers lost their seats. By then Upper Canada had a new, more competent governor, Sir John Colborne, so people weren't as upset as before. Mackenzie, however, still found plenty to be upset about. Instead of concentrating on major problems such as the need for more roads and schools in rural areas, shady deals behind the building of the Welland Canal, or the Bank of Upper Canada's protection from competition, he got equally angry about every little thing that bothered him.

In December 1831, the Tory majority voted to have Mackenzie thrown out of the assembly. That made the little man with the bright red wig look like David fighting Goliath. The day he was expelled, hundreds of people barged into the legislature in protest. A few weeks later, in a by-election to choose his replacement, Mackenzie won all but one vote. His supporters gave him a victory parade and a gold medal that would become his most prized possession. Five days later, the Tories foolishly voted to expel him again.

Mackenzie was re-elected again, but Tory opposition to him grew even stronger. In Hamilton he was mugged, and in York he was pelted with garbage and a riot broke out. Mackenzie had to hide out until arrangements were made for him and his wife to sail for England. He spent the summer of 1832 telling government officials in London about the Reformers' complaints, and they took him seriously. Governor Colborne was told to make sure Mackenzie was allowed back in the assembly, and to start making changes in how things were done in Upper Canada. But the Tories weren't about to take orders from England. In their own way, they were as independent-minded as Mackenzie was. They voted to expel Mackenzie again while he was away, and let him take his seat only when Governor Colborne made them do it.

In March 1834, York officially became a city and was renamed Toronto. Mackenzie ran in Toronto's first elections and became its first mayor. He brought in taxes to pay for things like paved roads and street lighting, and acted fairly as the city's court judge. But he was as hot-headed as ever, and handed out city jobs to his followers much as the Tories had to theirs. Just seven months after becoming mayor, he dove back into the whirlpool of provincial politics. Again, he and the Reformers won big, but try as they might, they couldn't get needed changes past the executive council and the province's new governor, Sir Francis Bond Head.

Feeling more and more desperate, Mackenzie even turned against some fellow Reformers. He received a real blow to his pride when he lost his assembly seat in the next election, held in 1836. Claiming the Tories had bought their votes, he started another newspaper, the *Constitution,* in which he could vent his fury. When colonial officials passed new rules making it impossible for the elected assembly to control the executive council, Mackenzie started hinting in his newspaper that people might have to take up arms against the government. This was a scary thought even for Mackenzie, but the more meetings he attended and the more he talked with like-minded reformers (Patriotes) in Lower Canada (Quebec), the closer he came to favouring an all-out revolt.

The rebellion, when it came, was a disaster. In the first week of December 1837, hundreds of men, led by Reformer Samuel Lount, began gathering north of Toronto at Montgomery's Tavern. Mainly farmers, they were poorly equipped and somewhat disorganized. Mackenzie tried to get Lount's group to hold off until December 7, the date of a planned show of force. But on the night of December 5, the rebels started marching down Yonge Street. They soon ran into a group of about twenty well-armed civilian guards who began shooting at them. Two rebels and one guard were killed, and the rebels retreated. The next day, a force of at least a thousand loyalists marched up to Montgomery's Tavern and sent the rest of the rebels running.

Mackenzie and a few other rebel leaders escaped to the United States, but that didn't end the conflict. With American support, Mackenzie took over Navy Island in the Niagara River and declared it a free Canadian republic. From there he hoped to launch new attacks to free Upper Canada from British rule. But cold weather and dwindling supplies forced him to abandon the island on January 14, 1838. He spent the next twelve years in exile in the U.S., taking odd jobs and writing for and running newspapers to get by. In 1849, he was finally allowed to return to Toronto.

By then, Mackenzie was poorer than ever, but when his friends got him a job as Toronto's postmaster, he turned it down. There was no way he was going to take a government job arranged for by well-connected friends. Instead, he started another newspaper and ran in the next election, this time for a seat in the Parliament of the province of Canada, formed when Canada West (Ontario) and Canada East (Quebec) were united in 1841. He continued to expose government corruption and to fight for the province's poor, but he eventually lost touch with his constituents' needs and became something of a laughing-stock when he made speeches in Parliament.

In 1858, tired, weak, in debt and totally frustrated, Mackenzie resigned from government. Friends set up a fund to raise money for a furnished house for him and his family, and he spent the final three years of his life there, enjoying some sort of comfort at last. Apart from his political failures, his only other regret was that he had once been so desperate for money that he'd had to melt down and sell the gold medal his supporters had given him. In August 1861, he had a seizure and went into a coma, and on August 28 the little rebel lost his last fight. Both the Tory and Reform newspapers of the day marked the passing of an honest man.

# Louis-Joseph Papineau
## 1786–1871

AT TIMES, trying to understand what Louis-Joseph Papineau stood for was like trying to catch the wind. Just when people thought they had figured out what he believed in, he seemed to change his mind. But at a time when so many French Canadians were struggling to get by, he was the man they chose to follow, in the hope that he would know best how to improve their lives in Lower Canada (Quebec). Many of them would even follow him into open rebellion.

There were a lot of problems in Lower Canada in the early 1800s. The fur trade was dying, wheat production was down, imported wheat from Upper Canada (Ontario) and the United States was more expensive, and the growing lumber business was making only a few people rich. Most people lived on small farms they rented from seigneurs, or major landowners, and they were barely growing enough crops and raising enough livestock to take care of their own families.

As times got tougher, seigneurs felt they needed more money, so they raised tenants' rents and started demanding money up front from people who wanted to clear and settle seigneurial land. Sons could no longer afford to start farming near their parents' land, and some of them moved to the United States, where land was cheaper and there were more jobs. However, new immigrants from Britain started arriving in greater numbers to take available jobs or set up their own businesses. That almost all these new-comers spoke English worried many French Canadians. So did the fact that they were often sick with cholera by the time their ships landed.

Frustrated by these and many other problems, people blamed the immigrants, the rich French and English business owners, and the province's government for their troubles. So when men like Papineau came along, eager to change how the government was run, people paid attention. Interestingly, though, Papineau was himself the son of a seigneur and his family was quite well-off. His parents had sent him to college, first in Montreal and then in Quebec, where teachers thought he was very smart but not a very hard worker. While at college he gave up the Catholicism of his strictly devout mother and of most French Canadians at the time.

When he graduated, Papineau began training to become a notary like his father. But he soon changed his mind, deciding that he didn't want to draw up deeds and wills and witness legal documents for the rest of his life. Instead, he began to study law, and even though he didn't like it very much either, he became a lawyer in 1810. By then he was also a politician. A year earlier, he had run for and won election to the legislative assembly as a member of the Parti Canadien.

Started in 1806, this party was made up mainly of middle-class French Canadians. They didn't like how the governor appointed mainly rich, English-speaking merchants to the legislative council. These appointees controlled government spending and made sure their relatives and friends got well-paid government jobs. Like the Family Compact in Upper Canada, they seemed to act like a gang of castle-dwelling nobles lording it over poor peasants. That's why they were nicknamed the Château Clique. At first, Papineau didn't want to change things too much. He just wanted the Château Clique replaced by French Canadians who would be willing to carry out the wishes of the elected assembly and would spread those good government jobs around more.

When the War of 1812 began, Papineau didn't want the Americans to take over Canada and make it a republic like the United States, or like France after its revolution. He liked the British form of government, with a monarch bound by a constitution to serve the will of the people. So, like many other French Canadians, he put aside his differences with the English and became a militia captain, ready to fight to defend his country. After the war, though, it was politics as usual. In 1815 he was elected Speaker of the assembly and also became the leader of the Parti Canadien. He remained Speaker until 1823, and served in that position again from 1825–32.

In 1817, when Papineau bought his father's vast property around Montebello, west of Montreal, he became one of those people whom the merchant class and many farmers wished would disappear—the seigneurs. Critics of the seigneurial system, including other political leaders such as Louis-Hippolyte LaFontaine (see p. 189), blamed it for holding back the agricultural development of the province and for reserving land ownership for a privileged minority. But Papineau thought that the system should stay as long as it kept land in French-Canadian hands. He didn't mind profiting from the labours of his tenant farmers either. His role as a seigneur and his effective but rather lofty speeches worried some fellow politicians, who would have liked him to keep in closer touch with the people he represented.

Nevertheless, people listened to Papineau when he objected to government abuses such as having people on the payroll who didn't do anything, giving pensions to dead people and paying annual salaries to people who didn't even live in the province. In 1818, the same year that he married Julie Bruneau, Papineau demanded that such abuses end, but he was ignored. In 1819, under his leadership, the elected assembly refused to approve funds for such things, but the appointed council approved them anyway.

Time and again the governor and his Château Clique friends ignored the assembly's complaints and did whatever they wanted. In 1822, they secretly asked the British Parliament to pass a law uniting Lower and Upper Canada. That move infuriated Papineau, who went to London to oppose it. He saw it as a plot to lessen the influence of French Canadians. The law wasn't passed, but the very thought of it added to tensions in the province. So did a scandal in 1824, when the government's paymaster was found guilty of using and losing what amounted to at least $300,000 of government funds.

Nearly a hundred thousand people signed petitions asking for reforms, and in the late 1820s officials in England agreed that changes were needed. But they were very slow in coming. By 1832, Papineau had changed his mind. He now wanted the legislative council to be elected and preferred the American form of government. The Catholic Church didn't like the idea of a republic because it gave more power to the people and might make them want to throw off the control the Church had over their lives. In the mid-1830s, when Papineau and other leaders started talking about revolting against the government if changes weren't made, Church leaders warned everyone not to listen to them. But Papineau's powerful speeches were stirring up angry feelings, and people started talking seriously about fighting for change.

Papineau didn't really want a violent rebellion, but he figured that the threat of it was the only way to make the governor see how serious the problems were. In 1837, however, the government rejected the major demands for change the Patriotes (the new name for the Parti Canadien) had made, and people started holding protest meetings throughout the province. Papineau rushed from one meeting to another, making speeches and meeting with other leaders, but when fighting finally broke out at St-Denis in November 1837, Papineau was nowhere to be found. Led by others such as Jean-Olivier Chenier, hundreds of poorly armed and somewhat disorganized French-Canadian rebels kept battling British troops and English-Canadian militias, but they were badly beaten, and many of their homes were looted and burned.

Papineau and several other Patriotes escaped to the United States. Some rebel leaders were furious with Papineau for not staying to fight, and they privately accused him of being a coward. Late in 1838, the Patriotes tried to breathe new life into their cause by attacking government troops again, but this time they were crushed. Nearly a thousand people were arrested, and there was more looting and burning. A dozen Patriotes were hanged and five dozen were sent to Bermuda and Australia and banned from returning.

Papineau was one of those who couldn't come back. He'd be arrested and imprisoned if he did. In February 1839, he sailed from New York for France. He, his wife and three children lived there until 1843. Then his family returned to Canada without him. He was pardoned in 1844, but it was only after a lot of prodding from his wife that he finally came back in 1845. By then, Lower and Upper Canada had been united into one province of Canada and renamed Canada East and Canada West, a situation Papineau hated. He had been against such a union ever since it was first proposed in 1822. Still, friends pushed him to run for office again, and in 1848 he did and was elected to the legislature. But he disagreed with his party's leader, LaFontaine, who was doing everything he could to make the new union work well for French Canadians. Papineau, the man who had led a militia in 1812, now said that if Canada East couldn't be independent, it should join the United States.

In 1854, Papineau decided he'd had enough of politics. He began spending more time at Montebello and became a very hands-on seigneur. His family wasn't thrilled about living in the country, so he built a huge mansion there that a few people mockingly referred to as his castle, or château. Unfortunately for him, his wife and children weren't impressed, and he spent a lot of time alone there, still defending the seigneurial system and supporting annexation to the United States.

After his death in 1871, people praised Papineau's leadership, but some still had trouble painting a clear picture of what he had stood for. Perhaps that was because he'd had trouble doing that himself at times. However, no one doubted for a second that he had loved his country with a passion and had always done what he thought best for his fellow French Canadians. He was there for them when they needed him most.

# Josiah Henson
## 1789–1883

JOSIAH HENSON was the youngest of six children born to slaves working for a farmer in the American state of Maryland. When Henson was about three or four years old, his father came home one day covered with blood. His back was slashed to ribbons and the side of his head was bleeding. That was young Josiah's only clear memory of his father. Some years later, his mother explained what had happened that terrible day. The farmer's overseer, or man in charge of the slaves, had viciously attacked his mother. His father had gone to her defence, and had been punished according to Maryland law. Like any other slave who dared to fight a white man there, he was given one hundred lashes with a whip and his ear was cut off.

After this incident, Henson's father was sold to someone in

Alabama and his family never saw him again. With her husband gone, Henson's mother and her six children were sent back to her original owner, a doctor who was kind to his workers. But when the doctor died, his property, slaves included, had to be sold so the estate could be settled. Henson, his mother, two brothers and three sisters were all sold to different owners. After his mother begged and pleaded, her new owner, Isaac Riley, finally agreed to buy back Henson so she could at least have her youngest child with her.

Riley would not regret that decision. Henson grew up to be one of his strongest, most competent workers, and he served him faithfully for several years. Riley trusted him and eventually put him in charge of running the farm. Whenever he could, Henson kept back a small portion of the crops he harvested to make sure the other slaves were well fed. When he was eighteen, he was given permission to attend a local church service, and that experience changed his life. Henson had never heard a sermon before, and he wanted to learn more about the message of love and hope that Christianity offered. Soon after he became a Christian, and from then on, he became more aware of and angry about the cruelty and injustice of slavery. Eventually he began to preach the message of Christianity to his own people.

When he was about twenty, Henson was savagely beaten by another slave owner's overseer. His arm was broken and both his shoulder blades were smashed. Riley's wife did the best she could to set his splintered bones, but he spent five pain-filled months recovering from his injuries. Not realizing that his bones hadn't healed fully, he went back to work in the fields and again cracked both shoulders while trying to use a plough. For the rest of his life, Henson could never raise his arms above his head.

When he was twenty-two, Henson married a young slave girl named Charlotte, whom he had met at church. They would have twelve children, and would enjoy a long and happy marriage. But their life in Maryland came to an end in 1825 when Riley ran into financial difficulties and sent his slaves to his brother in Kentucky so they couldn't be sold to pay his debts. There, Henson became a Methodist preacher. In 1828, he was sent back to Maryland on business. Along the way, he preached many powerful sermons at white churches and raised nearly $500, more than enough to buy his freedom. In Maryland, he paid Riley $450 to have his family set free, but when he got back to Kentucky, he learned that the man he had served faithfully for more than thirty years had cheated him. Riley had kept his money and arranged for his nephew to sell Henson in New Orleans.

On the boat ride down the Mississippi, Henson was tempted to kill the nephew and run away. Only his religious beliefs stopped him from doing so. But before they reached New Orleans, the young man became very sick and Henson had to take him back to Kentucky. It was then that he decided to escape. He had a hard time convincing his wife that this was the only way they could give their children any hope for the future. She was afraid of being caught and punished, but finally agreed to take the risk. The Hensons' long, terrifying journey from Kentucky ended on October 28, 1830, when they crossed the Niagara River to safety and freedom in Upper Canada.

For the next three years, Henson supported his growing family by working for two farmers in southern Ontario. In exchange, he got a place to stay and either wages or a share of the crops and livestock. The first farmer, a Mr. Hibbard, also sent Henson's oldest son, Tom, to school. After getting over his feelings of embarrassment, Henson finally accepted Tom's offer to teach him to read. With that skill mastered, Henson could finally read the Bible himself. He became a more effective preacher, and also took on a leadership role among other black families who had escaped and settled in the area. He held meetings and began to talk about ways in which his people could become their own bosses instead of always working for others.

In 1834, Henson and several other labourers rented a large section of government land and started their own farms. Seven years later, he used some of his own savings and contributions from a generous American opposed to slavery to buy some land at Dawn, near what is now Chatham, Ontario. There Henson built a community where runaway slaves could find refuge and receive an education that would help them start new, productive lives in Canada.

The Dawn settlement had its own flour mills and sawmills, as well as facilities for making bricks and ropes. It was also home to what has been called Canada's first adult-education and technical-training school. The school, known as the British-American Institute, got financial support from various church groups and anti-slavery organizations. Over the years, Henson helped raise money for it by going on speaking tours in the northern United States and England. He also served as the pastor of the Methodist church at Dawn.

In 1849, with the help of a writer named Samuel Eliot, Henson published the story of his life. It seems that the tale of his horrifying experiences as a slave inspired the American novelist Harriet Beecher Stowe to write her popular novel *Uncle Tom's Cabin* a few years later. After Stowe's book came out, Henson began to give lectures on his life as the "real Uncle Tom" on whom Stowe had based her novel's hero. But around the same time, some of the people who helped run Dawn accused Henson of doing a poor job overseeing the institute and handling some of the community's funds. One official successfully sued Henson over how he dealt with the sale of some property.

Nobody seemed to be able to solve the problems and the

in-fighting at Dawn, and the community eventually died out in the late 1860s. Henson remained in the area, preaching, writing and continuing to speak out against slavery until his death in 1883. His home at Dresden, Ontario, is now a museum that serves as an inspirational reminder of what life was like for the many blacks who managed to escape the fate of Henson's father and make new lives for themselves in southern Ontario.

# James Douglas
## 1803–1877

WHEN SIR JAMES DOUGLAS stepped down as governor of British Columbia in 1864, he told friends that nothing would make him prouder than to be remembered as someone who had done his duty. Douglas deserved to be remembered that way. A strong sense of duty guided him throughout his life. But there were times when he had to struggle with shifting or divided loyalties. Then it wasn't so easy to see where his duty lay.

In 1821, Douglas was an enthusiastically loyal employee of the North West Company (NWC). He'd just been sent to a NWC trading post at Île-à-la-Crosse in what's now northwestern Saskatchewan. There, he did even more than duty demanded of him. Sometimes he and three other Nor'Westers paraded like soldiers in front of a nearby Hudson's Bay Company (HBC) post to intimidate their rivals. His superiors told him to stop being so aggressive, but privately they were pleased to see how competitive he was.

Douglas even fought a duel with an HBC trader while he was in Île-à-la-Crosse. Fortunately, neither man was hurt, and a few months later, they were no longer rivals—the North West Company joined the Hudson's Bay Company, and Douglas suddenly found himself working for what had been the competition. After the merger, though, his duty was clear. He would become a Hudson's Bay Company man through and through.

Douglas was just sixteen when his father arranged for him to become a North West Company apprentice. John Douglas was a successful Scottish merchant with investments in sugar plantations in British Guiana. He met James's mother there. She was the daughter of a white father and a black mother. John never married her, but he took good care of his West Indian family. The couple had three children, Alexander, James and Cecilia. James and Alexander were sent to a private school in Scotland, and also received private tutoring. James learned to read and speak French fluently from one of his tutors. His bilingualism would be a real asset when he moved to Canada and found himself dealing with French Canadians involved in all aspects of the fur trade.

James sailed for Quebec in May 1819. When he reported to North West Company headquarters in Montreal, he learned that he was being sent to Fort William (now Thunder Bay). The trip there, through rugged wilderness in a voyageur's canoe loaded with trade goods, was almost more adventure than he had bargained for, but he quickly settled into his new life at the trading post. He worked as a clerk and bookkeeper, and learned everything he could about the fur-trading business. He spent his spare time reading, something he loved to do all his life.

The following spring, Douglas was sent to Île-à-la-Crosse. After the merger, Douglas's new HBC bosses kept an eye on him, and they liked what they saw. In 1825, they let him run Fort Vermillion, on the Peace River, for the summer, and in 1826 they sent him to Fort St. James, on Stuart Lake. Fort St. James was the main HBC post in New Caledonia (now British Columbia). William Connolly was in charge there. He was also the chief factor, or senior officer, of the whole New Caledonia region. Connolly liked and trusted Douglas and put him to work right away, transporting valuable loads of furs from the Upper Fraser River down to the mouth of the Okanagan River. The next spring, Connolly sent him 200 kilometres north to build a new trading post at Bear Lake.

Douglas was very lonely at Bear Lake. He had only a couple of books to read, and over the winter he nearly ran out of food. Native people in the area weren't very friendly either. They didn't like the idea of having a new fort in their territory. Douglas was seriously thinking of quitting when three things happened to change his mind. In the spring of 1828, he was offered a 40 percent pay raise, he was moved back to Fort St. James, and Amelia Connolly agreed to become his wife. She was the daughter of the chief factor and his Cree wife, Suzanne.

Like her mother, Amelia was married according to what was called "the custom of the country." This meant that without clergy around to perform wedding ceremonies, a couple got approval from the bride's father and simply agreed to be married. But unlike her mother, Amelia married a man who would never leave her. When Connolly moved back to Montreal, he claimed that his twenty-eight-year marriage to Suzanne wasn't legal, and he got married again, this time in a church and to a non-Native woman from Montreal. Douglas, however, never doubted that his marriage to Amelia was legal. He was always a loving husband and father. He and Amelia had thirteen children, but only six survived infancy.

In 1830, Douglas was moved to Fort Vancouver and promoted to accountant for the region. By 1839, he had worked his way up to chief factor, and was given temporary charge of Fort Vancouver. George Simpson, governor of the HBC, was very impressed with him, and often sent him on important missions for the company. He worked out a division of territory with the Russians operating trading posts to the north, and arranged trading rights with the governor of California to the south. He chose the site for a new post on the south end of Vancouver Island, and began building Fort Victoria in 1843. He was also named its new governor.

When the forty-ninth parallel, or line of latitude, was chosen as the new boundary between Canada and the United States in 1846, Douglas figured out new transportation routes for the HBC and moved its Columbia River headquarters north to Fort Vancouver. Three years later, Britain gave the HBC control of Vancouver Island for ten years in return for a promise to start settling the island. Douglas was disappointed when he wasn't chosen as the new colony's first governor. But he had plenty to do at Fort Victoria, maintaining peace in the area, paying what Natives at the time considered a fair price for lands the HBC took over and trying to come up with ways to keep out Americans who appeared to be eager to move north into British Columbia.

The island's new governor, a lawyer from England named Richard Blanshard, stayed only a year or so. When he resigned in 1851, Douglas took his place. He was now wearing two hats—as governor and as HBC chief factor—and that didn't always feel comfortable. The company kept making money, but there was no public money for things the entire region needed, such as roads, schools, police, a militia, judges and government buildings.

Douglas kept writing to HBC officials asking them to send out more settlers, teachers, schoolbooks and so on. He, in turn, tried to find ways to raise money locally. Early on, for instance, he made anyone wanting to sell alcohol pay for a liquor licence, and later he charged gold miners a licensing fee.

In 1856, Douglas received instructions from London to hold elections for an assembly to help run the colony. He wasn't sure that was such a good idea. An assembly wouldn't care too much about HBC concerns. Besides, he didn't think most people on the island were qualified enough to vote. Still, his duty as governor was clear. He arranged for elections to take place as soon as possible, and the island's first assembly met that August. He had allowed only men who owned a fair bit of property to vote, but he felt a certain pride in knowing that by then the colony had grown to the point that seven representatives were elected from four districts—Victoria, Esquimalt, Nanaimo and Sooke. Two years later, he felt even greater pride when his brilliant plan to build a road from Harrison Lake to Lilloet, up into the Fraser River goldfields, was a success.

Douglas also beefed up defences and expanded a naval base at Esquimalt. He encouraged African Americans who had come north to join a black militia unit and he appointed Native judges. When the lure of Fraser River gold brought a tidal wave of people to the area, he claimed the territory as crown land and did what he could to maintain order there. Then Britain decided to end the HBC's control over New Caledonia, and in 1858 mainland British Columbia became a new British colony.

Douglas was asked to take on new duties as its governor too, but only if he resigned from the HBC. Even though the pay wasn't very good, Douglas agreed. By then, he was feeling a stronger sense of duty to the colonies and their people than he was to the HBC. It would be a relief not to have to worry all the time about avoiding conflicts of interest. He was sworn in as British Columbia's first governor on November 19, 1858.

Douglas had never taken time off when he worked for the HBC. Now he had even less time to himself. He established the colony's new capital at New Westminster. From 1861 to 1863, he devoted a great deal of time and energy to the building of the great Cariboo Road, up the Fraser River canyon all the way from Yale in the south to Barkerville in the north. The route up the Fraser and along the Cariboo Road became the major transportation route for the prospectors, merchants and settlers who kept flowing into British Columbia.

In 1863, Douglas was disappointed to learn that he was going to be replaced as governor in 1864, one year before his six-year appointment was up. Residents of Vancouver Island and British Columbia were demanding a more democratic form of government, and officials in London thought it was time for a change. Douglas was worried that people would think he was being replaced early because he hadn't done a good job, so he was very pleased when Queen Victoria knighted him for his many years of service. That meant a lot to him before he stepped down in May 1864.

After decades of doing his duty, Sir James Douglas finally had some time to himself. He toured Europe. He spent time with a married daughter living in Scotland. In London he visited the graves of writers whose work had kept him company over the years. He toured galleries and museums, making notes on all he saw. When he returned to Victoria, he welcomed the chance to be with his wife, children and grandchildren. He skipped rope to stay fit, worked in his garden, read his books and kept a diary. Free of many of the burdens of duty, he took great pleasure in being a private citizen and a family man.

Douglas made his last diary entry on the morning of August 2,

1877. Later that day, he complained of pains in his chest. That evening, while talking with a son-in-law, the Father of British Columbia died of a heart attack. At Douglas's funeral, the Anglican bishop spoke for most British Columbians when he summed up his life by saying that "the right man was in the right place." And just as he had hoped, Douglas was remembered as one who was there when duty called.

# Louis-Hippolyte LaFontaine

## 1807–1864

FTER THE 1837 rebellions led by William Lyon
Mackenzie (see p. 164) in Upper Canada (Ontario)
and Louis-Joseph Papineau (see p. 171) in Lower
Canada (Quebec), Britain sent a new governor-general to its
colony. John George Lambton, the earl of Durham, was given
the job of trying to figure out exactly why people were so upset
with the government and seeing what could be done to calm
them down. When he arrived in 1838, he spent nearly six
months travelling around the colony and meeting with people
from all walks of life. He listened to their complaints and
to their suggestions for fixing problems. Then, in January 1839,

he wrote a report based on what he had seen and heard.

In his report, Lord Durham made two main recommendations. He said that Upper and Lower Canada should be combined into one province, a united Canada made up of Canada West (Ontario) and Canada East (Quebec). He also said that the new province's government should be responsible to the people, or do what a majority of its elected representatives wanted. The government would still be headed by a governor-general appointed by Britain, along with an executive council and law-making or legislative council appointed by the governor. However, the elected assembly would now be made up of forty-two representatives from Canada East and forty-two from Canada West.

Many French Canadians hated the thought of being forced into a union with Upper Canada. Papineau had been fighting that idea since 1822. His right-hand man, Louis-Hippolyte LaFontaine, had felt the same way when he was in his early twenties. But by 1839, Papineau was living in exile in France and LaFontaine was a more mature, wiser politician. He could still see the dangers a union might bring. After all, Lord Durham had come right out and said that he thought Canada would work better if French Canadians were assimilated, or began to speak, think and act more like the English majority in the country. Nevertheless, LaFontaine believed strongly in responsible government, and he thought French Canadians could make it work for them.

LaFontaine was the son of a carpenter from Boucherville, Lower Canada. He had sailed through his primary education and headed off to the Collège de Montréal at just thirteen. There, classmates dubbed him "the Big Brain" because of his great marks and his amazing memory. He was also very athletic and did well in all sports, especially tennis. He left college as soon as he could, went to work as a law clerk and became a lawyer when he was just twenty-one. When he was twenty-three, he married Adèle Berthelot, the daughter of a wealthy lawyer and politician. The LaFontaines loved children but could never have any of their own. They were devastated when their adopted daughter, Corrine, died when she was just thirteen.

LaFontaine quickly earned a reputation as a brilliant, dedicated young lawyer and as someone with a keen interest in politics. In 1830, the year before he got married, he ran for a seat in the elected assembly of Lower Canada. He won easily, and became Papineau's biggest supporter, working very hard for government reform. However, when the threat of violence became a real possibility in 1837, he did everything he could to head it off through peaceful, political means. Just before the rebellion began, he tried but failed to talk the governor-general into ending his suspension of the elected assembly so people could fight with words instead of fists and guns. After the fighting started, he went to England to see if he could get support from reform-minded politicians there for improving how Lower Canada was governed.

LaFontaine returned to Montreal in June 1838. There he joined his wife in her efforts to help the families of rebel leaders who were in jail or in hiding. While he was gone, she had been doing what she could to make sure that they were getting by on a day-to-day basis. Now, he started acting as the rebels' lawyer, working to get them pardoned. He helped convince Lord Durham that they could never get a fair jury trial, and that a pardon from the governor-general would go a long way towards calming things down. He had a lot to do with getting a pardon for some of them in 1838, and a final pardon of those still living in exile in 1845.

In November 1838, when more fighting broke out between other rebels and government forces, LaFontaine was one of several political leaders thrown in jail for a few weeks. He was released in December without any charges being laid against him, and went right back to looking for a peaceful way to make the government listen to the concerns of the people. When Lord Durham released his report early in 1839, LaFontaine thought he had found a way.

It took a lot of courage for LaFontaine to support the report, especially when the British Parliament agreed to the union of Upper and Lower Canada but refused to approve Durham's proposal for responsible government. LaFontaine also didn't like the fact that even though Canada East had more people than Canada West, it wouldn't get more seats in the elected assembly. What's more, when the Union Act became law in 1841, English became the only official language of the government, the capital was moved from Montreal to Kingston and the new governor-general, Lord Sydenham, didn't seem very sympathetic towards the concerns of French Canadians. Most of them were very upset by the unfairness of these changes. So was LaFontaine, but he had a plan.

LaFontaine's plan was to work with leaders in Canada West who were also angry and disappointed that Britain had rejected responsible government for Canada. They knew that as long as the governor-general and his appointed council could refuse to do what the majority of assembly members voted for, Canada's government still wouldn't be responsible to the people. LaFontaine and leaders such as Francis Hincks and Robert Baldwin (see p. 197) in Canada West decided to form a party of both French- and English-speaking reformers who all wanted responsible government. If a majority of reformers won seats in the House of Assembly, they could keep voting for changes and the government would eventually have to go along with them.

LaFontaine wasn't a powerful public speaker. He had little charm and no sense of humour. But he explained his reasoning calmly and clearly, and managed to convince several other French-Canadian politicians that his ideas made sense. However, by doing so, he put his political career and his personal reputation on the line. If his plan failed, many people would never forgive him, and he would never forgive himself.

In the 1841 election, tempers ran high at candidates' meetings and political rallies. In LaFontaine's own riding of Terrebonne, a huge crowd armed with clubs and guns stopped his supporters from voting. Rather than have a riot break out, he withdrew from the race. He probably would have lost anyway, because the opposing candidate had the backing of both the governor-general and many Patriotes opposed to the Act of Union. But just when it looked as if he would have to leave the fight for responsible government in the assembly to other reformers who had won their seats, Robert Baldwin came to the rescue.

Baldwin was the Reformers' leader in Canada West, and in September 1841, he arranged for LaFontaine to run in a by-election in York (now Toronto). With Baldwin's support, LaFontaine won a majority from the English-speaking voters of York. This impressive act of French–English co-operation marked the beginning of a life-long friendship between the two men. LaFontaine would return the favour in 1843, when Baldwin lost his seat and LaFontaine arranged for him to run unopposed in Rimouski, Canada East.

Governor-General Sydenham died in September 1841. The British colonial office warned his replacement, Sir Charles Bagot, not to cave in to the Reformers' demands and not to appoint French Canadians as ministers in charge of different government departments. But Bagot, who spoke fluent French, wanted to reassure French Canadians that the united government could work well for them. Besides, in 1842, there was a majority of elected Reformers in the assembly, including their two powerful leaders, LaFontaine and Baldwin. If they wanted to, they could call for and win a vote of non-confidence in Bagot's government. So he gave

LaFontaine the job of attorney-general for Canada East and Baldwin the same job in Canada West.

Even though LaFontaine could speak English, he purposely gave his first speech to the new assembly in Kingston in French. Speakers had been using both French and English in the Lower Canada assembly before the Act of Union, and he felt they should still be able to. It would take him six more years to get that part of the act changed. Still, he had plenty to do in the meantime. He improved the courts and justice system in Canada East, encouraged new settlement and agriculture in the Eastern Townships, got people thinking about ending the seigneurial system so more farmers could own their own land, and appointed many French Canadians to government jobs such as judges, school inspectors and postal officials. He also pressured Bagot's replacement, Governor Charles Metcalfe, into pardoning any exiled rebels who wanted to return home in 1845.

Papineau returned from exile in France in 1845, and began to argue with LaFontaine about his support for a united Canada. He wanted the Act of Union to be repealed, or cancelled. If that didn't happen, he thought Canada East should become an independent, American-style republic and join the United States. LaFontaine's reasons for remaining part of Canada won the day, and he and Papineau went their separate ways politically. But LaFontaine was very aware that it had been several years since Lord Durham had released his report, and the province of Canada still didn't have true responsible government.

Through all those years, LaFontaine had worked hard to build up a strong political party of reformers that could elect a majority in the House of Assembly, or Parliament, in the hope that a governor would approve the laws they passed. In 1847 a new governor, Lord Elgin, finally seemed willing to do exactly that. When the Reformers from Canada East and West won a large majority in the next election, held in 1848, Elgin asked LaFontaine and Baldwin to tell him who to appoint as cabinet ministers. Baldwin and the other members let LaFontaine act as their leader, so he in effect became the province of Canada's first prime minister. Better still, when Elgin read the speech from the throne, he did so in French and English, making both official languages accepted again.

All the ingredients of responsible government were now in place, but would they hold together? That's what LaFontaine wondered when the assembly passed the Rebellion Losses Bill in 1849. This bill allowed the government to repay residents in Canada East whose property had been destroyed during the 1837–38 rebellion. The assembly had approved similar payments for Canada West residents four years earlier. Even though convicted or exiled rebels wouldn't get money, English Tory, or conservative, members were furious at the thought that people who weren't loyal to Britain might get some. They also resented being controlled by the French-Canadian Reformers, who had a majority in government. The Tories angrily demanded that Lord Elgin refuse to sign the bill into law, and they threatened all sorts of trouble if he did.

In the past, governors would have backed down under such pressure, especially when it came from people loyal to British rule. But the assembly had passed the bill, so Elgin signed it into law. Afterwards, angry protesters pelted his carriage with stones and garbage when he moved through the streets of Montreal. Then a mob attacked the assembly building, which caught on fire and burned down. Rioters also destroyed LaFontaine's home and damaged the homes of other Reform leaders. But Lord Elgin held his ground and ordered troops to stay calm too, and peace eventually returned to Montreal without anyone being killed. And as LaFontaine had hoped, responsible government lived on too.

In the next year or so, LaFontaine began to find political life exhausting. A very honest man with high moral standards, he found it particularly difficult to try to deal fairly with the many requests to reward supporters with jobs or government appointment. By 1851, he was overweight, his rheumatism was getting worse and his wife was having rheumatism attacks too. That September, he submitted his resignation to Lord Elgin and, regretfully, Elgin accepted it.

In 1853, LaFontaine became Canada East's chief justice, or judge. His wife, Adèle, died in 1859, but he remarried in January 1861. This second marriage, to a widow named Julie (Jane) Morrison, brought him great joy. She already had three young daughters, and in January 1861 their first child, Louis-Hippolyte, was born. Sadly, he would never see his second son. His wife was four months pregnant when he died of a stroke on February 26, 1864. He was spared the pain of the premature deaths of both boys, in 1865 and 1867. But Canadians, French and English alike, deeply felt the pain of losing such an exceptionally intelligent, honest, dedicated leader. More than twelve thousand people turned out to show their respect for him on the day of his funeral.

# Robert Baldwin
## 1804–1858

ROBERT BALDWIN didn't really want to be a politician. He was a plain-looking, quiet young man who liked to write poetry. He was nervous making public speeches, and he worried a lot about making decisions. But his father was William Warren Baldwin, a lawyer from York (now Toronto) who was very involved in politics and believed that it was the duty of well-off, well-educated gentlemen to serve their country. He brought up his son to think the same way.

After finishing school at sixteen, Baldwin went to work in his father's law office, and then became a lawyer himself in June 1825. Nervous at first about arguing cases before a judge, he was pleasantly surprised to find that he did that very well. He really wanted to be a good lawyer, not just because he set very high standards for himself, but also because he wanted to impress Augusta Elizabeth (Eliza) Sullivan's parents. A few months before he'd been called to the bar and could start practising law, he and Sullivan had fallen in love.

She was his cousin, and she was just fifteen at the time, so her parents sent her off to stay with relatives in New York City for a while to see if their interest in each other would fade. But it grew stronger with each passing day. Shy and somewhat reserved in public, Baldwin wrote her passionate love letters in which he shared his deepest, most private thoughts, hopes and fears. He also wrote her some romantic love poems. Finally, both of their families approved of the match, and after more than a year apart, they were married in May 1827.

By then, Baldwin's father had become very outspoken about the need for responsible government in Upper Canada (Ontario). Although the province had an elected assembly, its members were powerless if the governor and his appointed councillors didn't approve of what they voted for. Baldwin agreed with his father, and felt duty bound to follow his example and get involved in politics too. In 1828, he ran for election but lost to a fiery opponent named William Lyon Mackenzie (see p. 164). In a way, he was relieved. His beloved wife was very sick during her first pregnancy, and he was happy to spend as much time as he could taking care of her. But he ran again in January 1829, and he won a seat in the House of Assembly as a Reformer committed to the fight for responsible government.

But Baldwin's early political career was short-lived. When King George IV died in June 1830, the government was dissolved and new elections had to be held. Baldwin lost a second time, and went back to just practising law for the next six years. Again, he didn't mind losing too much. By 1832, he and Sullivan had three young children, and he loved his life as a family man. Sadly, his wife had to have a caesarean section when their fourth child was born in April 1834, and she was very weak and sick afterwards. She never got better, and on January 11, 1836, she died, leaving Baldwin nearly in despair. He couldn't imagine his life without her, and he could never imagine a life with anyone else.

Later that January, the new governor, Francis Bond Head, asked Baldwin to be one of his appointed councillors. Baldwin turned him down, partly because he wasn't sure he could handle being back in politics, and partly because he had been very critical of some of the other councillors he would have to work with. When Bond Head asked him again in February, he decided to accept. He figured this would be the best way to see if Bond Head was really interested in making the changes people wanted in how the government was run.

One change all Reformers wanted was to stop having to approve payments for government jobs and pensions that all went to a few of the governor's rich and powerful friends known as the Family Compact. When Bond Head put off discussing responsible government with his new councillors in March, Baldwin and the others all resigned. A week later, the assembly refused to vote in favour of giving Bond Head the money needed to pay for those patronage jobs, so he suspended, or shut down, the assembly. After that, whispers of rebellion became loud chatter.

Baldwin wanted no part of violence. Instead, he went to England in the spring of 1836 to try to convince colonial officials that Canadians were entitled to the same sort of responsible government that people enjoyed in Britain. He didn't succeed, but he impressed people with how polite and reasonable he was. He spent the rest of the year touring England and visiting places in Ireland where his and Sullivan's ancestors had lived. He returned to Canada early in 1837, but he stayed out of politics then and knew nothing about Mackenzie's plans for the rebellion. After government forces crushed the rebels, he acted as the lawyer for many of them.

In March 1838, Lord Durham arrived as the new governor-general. He was the third governor sent to Canada since Baldwin had entered politics. Baldwin would end up trying to work with five more before finally achieving his goal of responsible government in 1849. However, he and his father were just two of the hundreds of people Durham met with to discuss complaints about the government and to look for ways to make Canada run more smoothly. By the end of the year, Durham had resigned, but in January 1839 he wrote a report that would change Canada forever.

What Baldwin liked most about Durham's report was the recommendation that Canada be given responsible government. Durham's other main recommendation was to unite Upper and Lower Canada into one big province with a single overall government. The new province would be called Canada, and Upper and Lower Canada would be known as Canada West and Canada East. Baldwin and a fellow Reformer, Francis Hincks, saw the union of the two provinces as a great opportunity to get the government changes they had wanted for so long, but only if French and English Reformers worked together. If they co-operated and got people to vote for candidates who wanted change, rather than for someone who spoke the same language or practised the same religion as they did, Reformers might be able to elect a majority in the new united House of Assembly.

Baldwin and Hincks contacted Louis-Hippolyte LaFontaine (see p. 189), the Reform leader in Lower Canada, and found that he had the same idea. What Baldwin and LaFontaine did, in effect, was to introduce the political party approach to election campaigns in Canada, and it worked well for them. The Act of Union went into effect early in 1841, and new elections were held in

March. Reformers in Canada East did better than those in Canada West, winning nearly half of their forty-two seats in the assembly. Baldwin's reformers managed to win only six of Canada West's forty-two seats.

But LaFontaine had been forced to withdraw from the race for his riding because of intimidation from English-speaking thugs supporting the new governor-general, Lord Sydenham. In the true spirit of co-operation, Baldwin arranged for his new French-Canadian friend to run in a by-election in York (now Toronto), and he helped LaFontaine get elected there. LaFontaine would do the same thing for him nearly two years later. When Baldwin lost his seat in Canada West in October 1842, LaFontaine invited him to run unopposed in Rimouski, Canada East.

After the 1841 election, Sydenham appointed Baldwin as one of his councillors, or cabinet ministers. But when he was sworn in, Baldwin refused to take the oath because part of it referred to the king as head of the Church and was insulting to Catholics, the majority of whom were French Canadian. This annoyed Sydenham, but he let Baldwin join his cabinet anyway. To further show how serious he was about making sure that French Canadians were treated fairly, Baldwin then told Sydenham that he must appoint four of them to his cabinet because they had won so many seats in the assembly. Sydenham refused, and then wrote a letter saying he accepted Baldwin's resignation as a councillor even though Baldwin hadn't resigned.

This dirty trick was almost too much for Baldwin. He wasn't sure he could last much longer in the cut-throat world of politics. But Sydenham died suddenly in September 1841, and his replacement, Sir Charles Bagot, seemed to be easier to get along with. Bagot appointed Baldwin attorney-general for Canada West and gave LaFontaine the same post in Canada East. However, when Bagot called a new election in the fall of 1842, Baldwin had a terrible time campaigning. Members of an anti-Catholic, very-loyal-to-England Protestant society known as the Orange Order harassed him everywhere he went and accused him of being a traitor to Britain and his own religion. He lost his seat and didn't get back into the assembly until LaFontaine arranged for him to run in Rimouski in January 1843.

The year 1843 was both good and bad for Baldwin. He managed to get pardons for some Upper Canada rebels, and got the capital moved back to Montreal. However, he failed to get approval for his plan to create a publicly funded university without links to any particular religion, and he got into serious trouble when he introduced laws to control secret societies like the Orange Order. In November 1843, an angry mob of Orangemen swarmed around his house and set fire to a stuffed figure that was meant to represent him. A few days later, when Bagot's replacement, Charles Metcalfe, insisted on keeping control of who got government jobs, Baldwin, LaFontaine and all but one other councillor resigned. They thought their resignations would force Metcalfe to change his mind.

Instead, Metcalfe adjourned the assembly and called another election in 1844, asking voters to show their support for British rule by voting against Reformers. The largely Protestant population of Canada West listened to him, and only eleven Reformers, including Baldwin, were elected there. Reformers still won a majority in Canada East, but overall they were outnumbered in the new assembly. Baldwin performed well in opposition, making some fine speeches about the need for responsible government and for Canadian-made solutions to Canadian problems. But neither Metcalfe, nor his successor, Charles Murray Cathcart, showed any sign of giving Canadians the chance to govern themselves.

However, just when Baldwin had begun to think responsible government was still a long way off, Cathcart was replaced by

Lord Elgin, and his instructions were to make sure that he and his appointed cabinet ministers did what the elected representatives voted for whenever possible. After new elections in 1848, the Reformers held more seats than the Tories, so Elgin asked them to choose his cabinet advisers, in much the same way that the winning party picks cabinet ministers today. This was a good sign, but the real test of Elgin's commitment to responsible government came when the assembly passed the Rebellion Losses Bill in 1849.

Proposed by LaFontaine and supported by Baldwin, this bill was intended to pay people in Canada East for property that had been damaged or destroyed during the 1837–38 rebellion. Convicted or exiled rebels weren't to get anything. Similar repayments had been made in Canada West in 1845, and it seemed only fair that French Canadians should get equal treatment. But most Tories were furious and saw the passing of the bill as a sign that French Canadians were bossing them around. They and a loud group of English-speaking Montrealers demanded that Elgin refuse to sign the bill into law. But Elgin signed it, because the assembly had passed it.

Baldwin's dream of responsible government had truly become a reality. Unfortunately, a very ugly scene followed the signing. When Elgin left the Parliament buildings, people threw things at his carriage. Then a large crowd burst into the assembly, smashed everything in sight and accidentally set the place on fire. Rioting went on for several more days, and Baldwin's rooming house was attacked. But Lord Elgin ordered troops not to use force unless absolutely necessary, and thanks to his leadership, calm eventually returned to the city without a single life being lost. Montreal was no longer the seat of government, however. Until Queen Victoria chose Ottawa as the permanent capital in 1858, the government took turns meeting in Toronto and Quebec City.

Baldwin stayed on in government for two more years, but his heart wasn't really in politics any more. Earlier in 1849, he had won approval of his University Bill, which created the University of Toronto. He had also made many improvements to the justice system in Canada West, an accomplishment of which he was quite proud. But his health was failing, and the bouts of depression he had suffered through for many years were lasting longer and getting much more severe. He had also become somewhat obsessed with death after his wife passed away, and his mother's death early in 1851 upset him greatly. At the end of June 1851, with tears in his eyes, he made his resignation speech to the assembly.

Baldwin spent the last years of his life struggling with depression, horrible headaches, terrifying dreams and strange thoughts of death. He had twice refused to let his older daughter, Maria, accept proposals of marriage, so she was still at home to take care of him. In 1854 his older son's wife, whom he really liked, died, and in 1858 his younger son came back home to live because he had been crippled by polio. It was all too much for Baldwin. He died on December 9, 1858, at his home in Spadina, on the outskirts of Toronto. His funeral four days later was the largest most Torontonians had ever seen. Thousands came out to honour the great political leader who had never really wanted to be a politician.

# Joseph Howe
## 1804–1873

JOSEPH HOWE was born in a cottage on the outskirts of Halifax, Nova Scotia. Like many other Nova Scotians, his parents, John Howe and Mary Ede Austin, were both United Empire Loyalists who left the United States after the American Revolution. John passed his great loyalty to Britain on to his son. He also passed on to him a love of reading. Much of Joseph Howe's early education came from reading the Bible and Shakespeare's plays together with his father and then discussing them with him. Howe had a great memory, and later on in life he would often weave quotes from Shakespeare into what he wrote and said.

The Howes didn't have much money, so they couldn't afford to send their son away to boarding school. But the local school was nearly a 4-kilometre walk away, so Howe didn't start going there until he was ten or eleven. And when he finally did, he was often called a dunce, or dummy. When he was thirteen, he realized he could learn more out of school than in, so he went to work in his father's printing shop in Halifax. His dad also ran the post office, so Howe often helped out there too.

Howe quickly learned the ins and outs of the printing business, but spending time with other young printers' apprentices, or trainees, taught him a few lessons his puritan parents wished he hadn't learned. As an older teen he hung out with a rougher crowd than they would have liked, but he was a hard worker and he continued to read late into the night. He also began writing poetry, and was very pleased when he was able to get some of his poems published. For a while, he even thought about trying to make a living as a writer. But when he was twenty-two, he and a nineteen-year-old friend bought the rights to a local newspaper, the *Weekly Chronicle,* and he suddenly found himself on the publishing side of the writing business.

Howe liked being a newspaper publisher. Later that year, he bought his own newspaper, the *Novascotian.* Just over a year after that, he married Catherine Susan Ann McNab. They would have ten children, only five of whom lived past childhood. But Howe was often away from home. He travelled throughout the colony and wrote about the things he saw and the people he met in rural and port communities. He also covered debates in the elected assembly, and learned a lot about government and politics while doing that. The more he saw of how government worked, the less impressed he was. He was particularly annoyed by how the governor and his appointed councillors could get their way, even when assembly members disagreed with them.

Like the Family Compact in Upper Canada and the Château Clique in Lower Canada, a small, powerful group of rich people were often able to stop the assembly from getting laws passed that would hurt their business interests. They usually made sure that their relatives and friends got government jobs too. Howe wanted the government to be more responsible, or to do more to make life better for ordinary, hard-working Nova Scotians. But in the early 1830s, he wasn't ready to join the ranks of outspoken Reformers calling for major changes in how the colony was run. He liked Nova Scotia's ties to Britain, and he didn't want to do anything to weaken them.

But that didn't mean he was willing to ignore corruption and abuses of power. In 1835, he published an unsigned letter from a reader claiming that for years local justice officials had been making money on the side by collecting extra fines from people. But he never bothered to check how true the charges were. He was sued for libel, or for publishing lies about someone that hurt his or her reputation. No lawyer wanted to defend him in court because it looked as if he was bound to lose, so Howe decided to defend himself. For six hours, he spoke non-stop and without notes on the importance of the freedom of the press and the need to feel free to expose corruption. The judge told the jury that Howe was guilty according to the law, but it took them less than fifteen minutes to find him not guilty.

Whenever he'd felt strongly about something, Howe's weapon of choice had always been words, but it wasn't until this trial that he realized how powerful they could be. As he left the courthouse, a cheering crowd picked him up and carried him through the streets to celebrate what they saw as a victory for the little guy.

The next year, Howe decided to fight for ordinary folks by running for election to the assembly. He didn't like the party approach to political campaigns that was becoming very popular in Britain and starting to take root in the colonies. He thought that a government run by one political party could boss people around just as much as a governor and his appointed advisers. Still, he ran as a Reform candidate, promising to improve a government that he compared with an ancient mummy all wrapped up in old, narrow ways of thinking, and he won easily in Halifax County.

Howe would have been happy simply with having people elect the legislative council members as well as the assembly members, and with the governor still having the final say. But when Lord Durham's report came out in favour of true responsible government for the colonies, with the governor having to go along with laws passed by a majority vote in the assembly, Howe supported this recommendation. However, he still wasn't willing to insist on this change as strongly as other Reformers were. In fact, after he was re-elected in 1840, he accepted an appointment to the executive council, even though there were anti-Reform Conservatives, or Tories, on it.

One Reformer was very upset with Howe for not giving his total support to the fight for responsible government, and he challenged him to a duel. Fortunately for Howe, the man missed, and even though Howe would have been justified in shooting the man, he shot into the air instead.

The assembly chose Howe to be its speaker, and he did his best to make the Reformers and Tories work together for the good of the people. But the governor listened more to his Tory advisers than he did to people like Howe, and he called a new election in 1843 in the hope that Reformers would lose their majority in the assembly. That happened, and when he chose mainly Tory members for the legislative council, Howe resigned from the council.

From then on, Howe became much more supportive of the Reform Party. He had sold the *Novascotian* back in 1841 so he'd have more time for politics, but after resigning he became the editor of two local newspapers. That way, he could write articles

criticizing the government and pushing for responsible government. In the next election, held in 1846, the only main issue was
responsible government, and the Reformers were back in the
majority in the assembly. The Tory government wouldn't resign, so
the assembly held and won a vote of non-confidence early in 1847,
and the new governor, Sir John Harvey, went along with that vote.
He asked Reformers to name his cabinet members, or councillors
in charge of various government departments, and he accepted
their leader, James Boyle Uniacke, as his first minister, or premier.

Nova Scotians now had responsible government, and as
Howe liked to brag, they hadn't needed a rebellion to get it. Of
course, the rebellions in Upper and Lower Canada had helped
Britain see the wisdom of finally listening to Lord Durham and of
telling Governor Harvey to accept the will of the people in Nova
Scotia. However, even though he had fought hard for the Reform
cause, Howe was passed over in favour of Uniacke to lead the first
responsible government in British North America. Howe had
written some very nasty, rude and even crude editorial columns
during the election campaign, and many Reformers had decided
he was too hot-headed to be the party's leader.

But Howe, not Uniacke, was the moving force behind many
of the new government's plans. He made sure that many Tories
were replaced with more liberal-thinking Reform supporters in
government jobs. He was on friendly terms with Harvey, and won
his support for many new projects. In the 1850s, he pushed forward his plan to build a railway across Nova Scotia, from Halifax
to Windsor, and when the railway project finally got underway in
1854, he became the chairman of the new railway board.

But Howe got into trouble too. In 1855, when Britain entered
the Crimean War, he slipped into New England to try to get
Americans to join the army and help Britain fight Russia. The
United States had declared itself to be neutral in this war, so what

Howe was doing was illegal, but he managed to talk his way out of being charged by American officials. By the time he returned to Nova Scotia, a new election campaign was nearly over and his new opponent, Dr. Charles Tupper, had been winning a lot of support while he was away. Tupper, a Tory, beat Howe, but the Liberals (mainly former Reformers) managed to hold on to their majority. Then Howe thoughtlessly said something insulting to Catholics that got most Liberal Catholic members of the assembly so angry they voted against their own party and supported the formation of a Tory government.

In the 1859 election, the Liberals squeaked back into power with just a three-seat majority, and after the new Liberal leader resigned to become Nova Scotia's chief justice, or judge, Howe finally became premier. But because he had such a small majority, he was always in danger of losing a vote of confidence to Tupper and his Conservatives. In 1862, he accepted an appointment from Britain as imperial fisheries commissioner. He had always wanted an appointment like that. He figured that Britain should treat its subjects in the colonies the same as people in Britain, and that citizens throughout the British Empire were equally entitled to British government appointments.

But many Liberal voters weren't impressed with Howe's new appointment. In the 1863 election, he lost his assembly seat and Tupper's Tories won a huge majority. Tupper tried to make peace with his old political foe by inviting him to be one of Nova Scotia's representatives at a conference being held in Charlottetown in September 1864, but Howe turned him down. It was at that Charlottetown meeting of leaders from Nova Scotia, New Brunswick, Prince Edward Island, Newfoundland and Canada (Canada East and Canada West) that plans for forming a new united, or confederated, country began to take shape.

Tupper was a strong supporter of this union, but Howe was

against it. He was afraid that Nova Scotia would lose its independence in such a confederation, and that Nova Scotians would end up having to pay high taxes to a central government that would spend them in other parts of Canada. He was also very upset that Tupper wouldn't let everyone vote on whether they wanted to join Confederation. Many people agreed with Howe, but he couldn't stop the Tory majority from voting in favour of Confederation. He even went to England to try to convince politicians there not to pass the British North America Act, which would create the new dominion of Canada.

When that failed, and Confederation became law on July 1, 1867, Howe decided to run in the new country's first elections and take his fight to Ottawa. In September 1867, Nova Scotia voters defeated all but two of the candidates who had supported Confederation. As a member of Parliament, Howe fought for Nova Scotia's right to pull out of the union, but it was too late. He even went back to London to ask for that right, but he failed. However, he did manage to get a better financial deal for Nova Scotia, and he finally accepted the fact that Britain wasn't going to change its mind.

In January 1869, Howe accepted a cabinet appointment from Canada's new prime minister, Sir John A. Macdonald (see p. 219). In November of that year, he travelled to Red River territory on behalf of the government to meet with the Métis leader Louis Riel (see p. 227). He tried but failed to convince Riel that he needn't be afraid of Canada's takeover of Rupert's Land. Three years later, exhausted by politics and in poor health, he accepted another appointment, this one from Britain.

In May 1873, he was sworn in as lieutenant-governor of Nova Scotia. He felt very honoured to have been chosen for this position, but he never got to enjoy it. Three weeks later, at home in the governor's residence, he died at the age of seventy-one.

# George-Étienne Cartier
## 1814–1873

**E** ARLY IN 1838, local newspapers reported that George-Étienne Cartier, a popular young lawyer from St-Antoine-sur-Richelieu, Lower Canada (now Quebec), had frozen to death. Cartier had disappeared at the end of November 1837, after taking part in fighting against government troops at St-Denis. He had been an enthusiastic supporter of Louis-Hippolyte LaFontaine (see p. 189) and his rebel Patriotes, who were fighting for responsible government in Lower Canada. People in neighbouring villages were sad to read of Cartier's death, but his family wasn't. They and a few Patriotes knew something no one else did—Cartier was very much alive, and was hiding out with his cousin in a local farmer's barn.

If Cartier hadn't flirted too much with the farmer's daughter, her boyfriend wouldn't have threatened to turn him in to the authorities, and he probably could have stayed on in the barn's attic for several more months. Instead, he had to slip into the United States in May 1838 and hide out there because he was one of many rebels charged with treason. In the fall, he was allowed back in Canada and managed to convince authorities that he hadn't acted like a traitor. Years later, he would explain his active involvement in the rebellion as simply youthful enthusiasm for a noble cause.

Cartier was the son of Jacques Cartier (not a descendant of the explorer), who had inherited a fortune from his merchant father and grandfather. But Jacques liked the good life, and spent so much of the family's money that his wife had to sue him for some of it before it was all gone. Although there was no legacy for Cartier to inherit, he did seem to inherit his father's love of lively songs, great parties, good food and fine wine. Still, when he went to college in Montreal, he didn't let his love of fun get in the way of his studies. He was an excellent student and won almost every academic prize offered at the college.

When Cartier graduated in 1831, he became a law clerk in the office of Éduard-Étienne Rodier, a Montreal lawyer who spoke out often against the way the government was run by a small, powerful group of individuals who were friends of the governor. Rodier encouraged his young law clerk's interest in politics, and in 1834 Cartier worked very hard to help Louis-Joseph Papineau (see p. 171) win election to Lower Canada's House of Assembly. He also joined the new St. Jean Baptiste Society and wrote some patriotic songs about his love for French Canada. He became a practising lawyer in November 1835, and soon had some well-established businessmen as clients. But that didn't stop him from becoming a Patriote supporter and becoming involved in the 1837 rebellion.

After he returned "from the dead" in 1838, Cartier spent the next ten years expanding his law practice. The practice did very well, and he invested his profits in property in Montreal. He also accepted appointments to the boards of banks and major companies, and became the lawyer for some clients involved in the growing railway business. When the Act of Union joining Lower and Upper Canada became law in 1841, he threw his support behind Louis-Hippolyte LaFontaine, who was determined to make the union work for French Canadians.

In June 1846, Cartier married Hortense Fabre, who came from a wealthy, influential Montreal family. They would have three daughters, but their marriage wasn't the happiest. Fabre found it hard to put up with Cartier's love of socializing with friends so much and of giving and going to parties so often. Around 1860, Cartier began a relationship with another woman, Luce Cuvillier, that would continue until he died. When Fabre and their daughters learned about Cuvillier, their relationship with Cartier became very strained.

In 1848, Cartier figured that his finances were in good enough shape that he could afford to enter politics. He ran for election in Verchères that year, and won a seat in the new assembly of the united Canada. Like so many others who had wanted responsible government, he was very happy when Lord Elgin asked LaFontaine and Robert Baldwin (see p. 197) to form the government, and he was thrilled when Lord Elgin returned French to its rightful place as an official language of government. But as the years went on, he became more conservative in his politics. He preferred a calmer atmosphere that would allow businesses to thrive in Canada East (Lower Canada before the Act of Union) and French Canadians to be better off.

But that didn't mean he wasn't prepared to fight for changes that might upset some people. He pushed for government financial support for the building of railways, set up a strong public school system for Protestants and Catholics in Lower Canada, and worked very hard to end the seigneurial system of holding land. He wanted more farmers to be able to own their own land so that they could breathe new life into the province's agricultural business, and he was happy to see the system end in 1854. He made some new enemies in Canada West (Upper Canada before the union) a couple of years later when he got the assembly to approve some extra payments to seigneurs for the land they'd given up. After becoming attorney-general for Canada East in 1856, he also made French civil (not criminal) law apply to all of Canada East, even in mainly English-speaking regions.

In 1857, Cartier became the leader of the Conservatives, or *bleus*, in Canada East, and late that year the governor-general asked him and Canada West's Tory leader, John A. Macdonald (see p. 219), to form a new government. Cartier and Macdonald made a great team. They also became very good friends. Officially, Macdonald was the first minister, or leader, of this government, but in effect he and Cartier were co-premiers. In August 1858, Macdonald resigned as first minister to protest an assembly vote against Queen Victoria's choice of Ottawa as Canada's new capital. Cartier took over as official leader, but after some tricky political manoeuvring, Macdonald was back as co-premier. However, in 1862 the entire Cartier-Macdonald government had to resign when the assembly voted against a plan to set up a large Canadian militia because it would cost too much.

Around this time, the call from Canada West for representation by population was getting louder, and Cartier was concerned. When Canada became one united province in 1841, Canada East and Canada West were given an equal number of seats in the elected assembly even though Canada East had more people. Now Canada West's population was higher, and many people there were saying this arrangement was unfair. Cartier said the system was fine because it had been part of the Act of Union. But privately, he figured it would be only a matter of time before Canada West got more seats and a mainly English majority would end up controlling the assembly and all French Canadians.

Because of his close ties with railway companies, Cartier could see that the provinces were going to become more and more connected. But he was afraid that if they didn't start cooperating more, they would be taken over by the United States, a thought that made his blood run cold. He was sure French Canadians would be swallowed up and disappear into the vast country to the south if that happened. But if Canada East and Canada West became separate members of a confederation, or cooperative union, with the Maritime provinces, Cartier thought French Canadians would be much better off. In 1858 he had gone to London with Alexander Galt and John Ross, two politicians from Canada West who also liked the idea of uniting the provinces, but British officials had decided the time wasn't right for such a union. When he was re-elected in 1863, he decided to work harder for it.

Cartier's chance to speak very strongly in favour of Confederation came at a conference held at Charlottetown, Prince Edward Island, in September 1864. Leaders from the Maritime colonies listened carefully to what he had to say, and they agreed to meet again at Quebec in October. This time he let John A. Macdonald present the Confederation plans the two men had discussed and worked out earlier in Canada's assembly. After many more discussions, arguments and debates, the provinces of Canada, New Brunswick and Nova Scotia worked out an agreement to form a new country, Canada, and Britain gave this agreement its blessing. At the time, Prince Edward Island and Newfoundland chose to remain independent British colonies.

In March 1867, the British Parliament passed the British North America (BNA) Act, creating the new country of Canada from Quebec, Ontario, New Brunswick and Nova Scotia. Each province was to have its own provincial government, and the country as a whole would have a government made up of representatives from each province. When the BNA Act went into effect on July 1, 1867, Lord Monck, the governor-general, introduced the new country to its first prime minister, Sir John A. Macdonald. Cartier was pleased to learn that his best friend had just been honoured by Queen Victoria with a knighthood, but he turned down a lesser reward that was offered to him. He wasn't jealous of Macdonald, but he felt that he had deserved an equal honour. The next year he was named a baronet, a title he felt he had earned.

Macdonald gave Cartier the cabinet post of minister of defence in the new government, and in 1868 he finally got approval for the Canadian militia he had wanted to establish six years earlier. Later that same year, he headed off to London to work out the details of an arrangement to make Rupert's Land and the North-West Territories part of Canada. He did a superb job during these negotiations, and returned home in the spring of 1869 with a deal that would greatly expand Canadian territory and lead to the formation of a new province, Manitoba, in 1870. He was also the person who negotiated with British Columbia and worked out the agreement that brought that colony into Confederation in 1871. A year later, in keeping with the promise to link B.C. to eastern Canada with a railway, he introduced the Canadian Pacific Railway Bill in Parliament.

But in August 1872, Cartier suffered his first election loss. Macdonald wanted him back in government as soon as possible, so an arrangement was made for him to run in September in the new riding of Provencher, in Manitoba. Cartier had supported the Manitoba Métis' fight for French-language rights and Catholic schools, and he wanted a pardon for Louis Riel (see p. 227), so Riel himself withdrew from the race in Provencher, leaving Cartier as the only candidate.

But Cartier was never to see the riding for which he was now a member of Parliament. At the end of September, he sailed for England to consult some doctors who specialized in treating a kidney disease he had learned he had in 1871. His wife and two of his daughters went with him and supervised his care and treatment in London, but he got worse and worse. On May 20, 1873, a telegram reached Canada with news that shocked the country. Sir John A. Macdonald was reduced to tears when he had to announce to Parliament the death of his best friend earlier that day.

The boat carrying Cartier's remains arrived in Quebec on June 9. After a special church service there, his coffin was returned to the ship and taken up the St. Lawrence River to Montreal for a state funeral. On the morning of June 11 bells rang out solemnly, soldiers and militia members stood in silent salute, and thousands of people lined the streets as the tall funeral carriage drawn by eight black horses moved along the route to Notre Dame church for funeral services. Politicians and dignitaries from every part of the country were there to pay their last respects. That afternoon, Cartier's body was laid to rest in the family plot in Côte-des-Neiges cemetery. Beside the open grave, Sir John A. Macdonald stood with tears streaming down his face. His tears were those of a friend and a prime minister mourning the loss of a truly great Canadian.

# John A. Macdonald

## 1815–1891

JOHN ALEXANDER MacDONALD was five years old when his parents, Hugh Macdonald and Helen Shaw, moved to Canada from Scotland. They came in the hope of making a better life for themselves and their four children. They settled in Kingston, Upper Canada (now Ontario), because Shaw had relatives living there, and Hugh Macdonald became a shopkeeper. After four years of losing money, Macdonald moved his family a little west of Kingston and started another shop. It failed too, so he moved the family again. After a third move and shop failure, he bought a grain-grinding mill about 9 kilometres from what's now Picton, Ontario. The Mackenzies called Stone Mills home for the next ten years.

Young Macdonald found it hard to keep moving like that.

Years later, he would say that he never really had a boyhood. When there wasn't a one-room schoolhouse within walking distance, his parents taught him at home. When he was thirteen, they managed to come up with enough money to have him stay at a boarding house in Kingston and attend a small private school there. He was an excellent student with a passion for reading, and he impressed his teachers with his quick mind and good behaviour.

In 1830, when he was just fifteen, he had to start earning his own living, so he went to work as a law clerk in Kingston. George Mackenzie, the lawyer he worked for, found him to be a very good worker and a fast learner, and after two years he put Macdonald in charge of his second office in nearby Napanee. Local townsfolk liked the well-read young man with the great sense of humour and the amazing memory for names and faces. These qualities, together with hard work and a friendly, down-to-earth way with people, would impress voters later when he entered politics.

By 1835, Macdonald had scraped together enough money to open his own law office in Kingston. He soon earned a reputation as a brilliant lawyer willing to take even the most difficult cases. He passionately believed in fighting for justice, no matter how unpopular the accused might be. But he wasn't a supporter of the rebels fighting for government reform in 1837. He hated corruption and was always willing to speak out against it, but he was loyal to Britain and didn't believe violence was the way to bring about change. When Americans threatened to support William Lyon Mackenzie (see p. 164) in 1838, Macdonald joined his fellow militiamen preparing to defend Fort Henry and Kingston against possible attacks from across Lake Ontario.

When Lord Durham's report came out in 1839, Macdonald didn't emerge as a strong supporter of responsible government. However, like many people in Kingston, he didn't like the way a few powerful people in Toronto seemed to have so much control over what the government did. He was fairly conservative in his political beliefs and was opposed to Reformers' demands for major changes in how the government was run, but he was quite prepared to criticize his fellow Tories to the west when they abused their power.

Macdonald's law business picked up a lot when Kingston became the capital of the new united province of Canada in 1841. He got to know some of the government officials and politicians looking for rooms or houses to rent in the new capital, and in 1843 he decided to enter the political arena himself at the local level, winning a seat on the city council. That same year he married Isabella Clark, a cousin he had met when he'd gone back to Scotland for a visit. He and Clark had two sons, but their first boy died just after his first birthday. Macdonald's joking manner in public would mask the sadness he felt when his son died and the helplessness that often weighed him down as his beloved Isa, as he called his wife, fought off illness after illness. Their thirteen-year marriage would end with her death in 1856.

In 1844, decked out in the brightly patterned vests that he loved to wear, Macdonald stood for election to the province of Canada's legislative assembly. Kingston voters gave him the nod and he proudly took his seat as their representative, marking the beginning of an incredible forty-seven-year political career. It also marked the beginning of a long struggle to stay out of debt. Politics would often take him away from his law practice, and campaign costs would eat away at his savings. But he thrived on debating important issues, and he loved having the chance to chat with his constituents and listen to their complaints.

It didn't take long for like-minded politicians to see Macdonald's leadership qualities. In 1847, he was appointed receiver-general of the province. But the various political groups that called themselves Conservatives were a divided lot, and when responsible government finally arrived in 1849, they had a hard time winning majorities against the well-organized Reformers. Macdonald worked hard to unite his Tories, and in 1856 he became their leader, but their support was still just coming mainly from English-speaking residents of Canada West (Ontario). Macdonald knew that his party had to gain support in Canada East (Quebec), but that was easier said than done. Votes in the elected assembly were often divided along language (French–English) and religious (Catholic–Protestant) lines, and it was very difficult for any one government to stay in power for very long.

Macdonald was convinced that only a strong Canada, respectful of language and religious differences, with ties to Britain that included a parliamentary-style government and British military support, could stop his country from becoming part of the United States. From 1856 to 1862, he served as co-premier of the province, first with Étienne Taché and then with George-Étienne Cartier (see p. 212), with whom he would form a life-long friendship. During that time, he pushed for co-operation among the various political parties so that they could all get on with the business of governing. But he often had to put off things he wanted to get done because he knew his bills wouldn't get majority approval in the rowdy, divided legislature. He was already beginning to earn one of his many nicknames, Old Tomorrow.

In 1862, his and Cartier's government went down to defeat when the assembly refused to pass a bill establishing a large, well-organized Canadian militia to fight beside British troops in case of an American invasion. (At the time, some Irish-Americans known as Fenians were talking about fighting Britain by attacking its colonies to the north.) In opposition, Macdonald became more and more fed up with all the political wrangling. He started drinking too much again, something he did whenever he felt miserable or hard done by, and by early 1864 he was seriously considering resigning as party leader. But later that summer, something happened to give him new hope for Canada's future.

Macdonald and Cartier were invited to a conference of leaders from the Maritime colonies in Charlottetown, Prince Edward Island. The conference had been planned to explore the possibility of forming some sort of co-operative Maritime union. When Cartier and Macdonald suggested a union of all the colonial provinces, including Canada East and Canada West, people seemed interested in discussing the possibility. After nearly two weeks of meetings in Charlottetown and Halifax, representatives from Canada, Nova Scotia, New Brunswick and Prince Edward Island agreed to meet again in Quebec City in October to discuss what might be involved in forming a larger co-operative union, or confederation.

From the fall of 1864 through to the winter of 1866–67, Macdonald worked tirelessly to finalize details of a federation that would shape the new country. Wanting to avoid the disastrous civil war that had recently torn apart the United States, he insisted on having a strong central government, with only certain powers going to the provinces. Leaders from Prince Edward Island and Newfoundland didn't like that idea and chose to have their provinces remain independent British colonies. But the other provinces were more open to this idea, and after much debate, and with the full support of Britain, the British North America Act was passed early in 1867. The new Dominion of Canada was finally officially born on July 1, 1867, with John A. Macdonald as its leader. Everyone who had worked with him over the previous two years agreed that he had earned the honour of serving as Canada's first prime minister. Queen Victoria honoured him too by making him a knight.

A few months earlier another woman, Susan Agnes Bernard, had honoured Macdonald by accepting his proposal of marriage. After years alone, he was going to Ottawa with a witty, smart, charming wife at his side. He and Bernard had one daughter, Mary, who was born physically and mentally handicapped. They showered her with love and care and, unlike some other parents at the time, made sure to include her whenever possible in the many social events they hosted.

Macdonald's years as prime minister were marked by many highs and lows. In 1869, he sent his friend Cartier to England to negotiate the Hudson's Bay Company's turnover of Rupert's Land and the North-West Territories to Canada. Cartier's mission was a great success, but Macdonald moved too quickly to assume control of the new territory. He never bothered to find out what the mainly French-speaking Métis settlers living in the Red River Valley thought about joining Canada. The Métis leader Louis Riel (see p. 227) said the government had to discuss the takeover with his people first. Only after fighting broke out between Riel's followers and some pro-Canada supporters did Macdonald's government take the time to work out terms for the new province of Manitoba to join Confederation in 1870.

Macdonald's government was also in power when negotiations brought British Columbia and Prince Edward Island into Confederation in 1871 and 1873, and it was his government that passed a bill in 1873 to form the North West Mounted Police (now the RCMP). His greatest accomplishment, however, was the building of the Canadian Pacific Railway linking Canada from east to west. But the railway was also the cause of his downfall in 1873.

During the 1872 election campaign, Macdonald accepted a large amount of money from Sir Hugh Allan, a businessman who wanted to win the contract to build the railway. In the spring of 1873, two pro-Liberal newspaper editors learned what Macdonald had done and wrote articles about what became known as the Pacific Railway Scandal. Accused of bribery and corruption, Macdonald resigned in disgrace, and the Liberals won the next election.

But Macdonald's Conservatives were back in power in 1878, and Macdonald was back in the prime minister's seat in the House of Commons. Old Reynard, as he came to be known because of his fox-like cleverness, won two more elections for the Conservatives and continued working as hard as ever for the country he loved with a passion. But no matter how busy he was, he always made time for his family. Time and again, he would slip away for an hour from late-night debates on Parliament Hill to read Mary a favourite story before she fell asleep.

During his last years in office, Macdonald had to deal with Riel again. He was unable to prevent the 1885 Northwest Rebellion in what is now Saskatchewan, and his refusal to spare Riel's life after he was convicted of treason infuriated many French Canadians in Quebec. That same year, he created Canada's first national park at Banff, Alberta, and celebrated the completion of the Canadian Pacific Railway (CPR). When he was seventy-one, he finally got to see most of the country he had helped build when he and Lady Agnes rode the CPR trains all the way out to British Columbia.

Macdonald lived to see the day in April 1891 when his son, Hugh, took a seat in the House of Commons as the newly elected member of Parliament from Winnipeg. But just one month later, he suffered a massive stroke. A week later, on June 6, 1891, the Father of Confederation was dead. Grief-stricken Canadians across the country went into mourning, but the mourning period didn't end with his impressive state funeral. His successor, John Abbot, wouldn't move into Macdonald's seat in the Commons, and the empty place served for just over a year as a daily reminder of the country's loss. When the House of Commons met on the first anniversary of his death, all the cabinet ministers and many of the members of Parliament wore roses in their lapels, and there was a huge rose bouquet on the clerk's table in front of the Speaker's chair.

When Macdonald campaigned for re-election the last time in 1887, many supporters had yelled out, "You'll never die, John A." They were right. Macdonald lives on forever in the history of Canada, and in the hearts of Canadians who celebrate that history.

# Louis Riel
## 1844–1885

O N DECEMBER 12, 1885, a quiet sadness filled the air around St. Boniface Cathedral in Winnipeg as the Métis community gathered for the funeral of Louis Riel. People had been waiting nearly a month to show their respect for this man who had been hanged in Regina. The line of mourners behind his casket stretched for nearly 2 kilometres.

The Métis—people of French and Aboriginal descent—weren't just burying one of their own. They were burying their leader, a man who had fought long and hard for their rights. And, many feared, they were burying with him their people's hopes and dreams for the future.

Born near St. Boniface, Manitoba, on October 22, 1844, Riel had learned early on how important it was for the Métis living in the Red River area to stand up for each other. His father had helped Métis hunters break the Hudson's Bay Company's monopoly, or total control, of the fur trade in the North-West Territories. Riel Sr. became a local hero, and his son would one day proudly follow in his footsteps.

Riel came from a close-knit, hard-working family. His parents, Jean-Louis Riel and Julie Lagimonière, had eleven children. Louis was their first-born. From a very early age, Lagimonière taught them all to say their prayers and took them to church every day. When he was old enough, Louis went to the local Catholic school, which was run by the Grey Nuns. The nuns were very impressed with him. He wasn't just a good student; he was also kind and generous. In 1858, he got a scholarship to attend college in Montreal.

Riel was very homesick at the Collège de Montréal, but he worked hard and soon was getting top marks. Over time, classmates came to respect this handsome, somewhat moody young man who loved to write stories and poetry and whose life was guided by his religious beliefs. He didn't drink, lie or cheat, and he was always willing to help out a friend. Once, he even nursed a fellow student with smallpox, a very contagious disease. Teachers at the college thought he would make a fine priest.

In January 1864, Riel received news that upset him terribly. His dad had died suddenly. He wished he could mourn with his family and worried about how they would manage without Jean-Louis. But later that year, he had something else on his mind—he'd fallen in love with a young woman named Marie-Julie Guernon.

In March 1865, Riel made a big decision. He knew that as a priest he wouldn't be able to help out his family and he would never be able to marry. So just four months before graduating, he decided to quit school. He found a job as a law clerk, but eventually saw that becoming a lawyer wasn't for him, nor was becoming Guernon's husband. Her parents didn't think he was good enough for her, and they forbade her to marry him.

In 1867, with nothing left for him in Montreal, Riel began the long journey home. He worked in the United States at odd jobs and finally made it back to St. Boniface in July 1868. Soon after, he bought some land beside the family farm, and began farming too.

It didn't take long for Riel to see that trouble was brewing in the area. After Confederation in 1867, more settlers were moving west, and many Protestant English-speaking newcomers from Ontario were showing strong anti-French, anti-Catholic and anti-Native feelings. What's more, the Hudson's Bay Company was about to sell control of a territory known as Rupert's Land to Canada, and Ottawa was planning to take it over without even asking people living there what they thought of the idea.

In August 1869, many Métis settlers became very upset when Canadian surveyors showed up and started staking out lands that belonged to them. By then, most of the buffalo were gone and beaver-pelt prices had dropped so low there wasn't much point trapping them any more. Were they about to lose their farms too?

The time had come to act. In October, Riel led a protest and the surveyors stopped work temporarily. Then he organized a council with two representatives from each parish. When the territory's newly appointed lieutenant-governor showed up at Pembina, just south of the Canadian border, Riel was ready for him. He sent William McDougall a message saying that he couldn't enter the Red River territory without the committee's permission. Then he led a bloodless capture of Fort Garry, the Hudson's Bay Company headquarters.

Soon several English and mixed-blood English-Native settlers joined the committee, and on December 1 Riel presented members with his plan for a new bilingual, elected government and a list of rights that would have to be protected before the territory joined Canada.

By then, Prime Minister John A. Macdonald (see p. 219) had decided that he had better delay the takeover. He sent a message to McDougall to stay put in Pembina until further notice. But McDougall didn't get the message in time, and he sent one of his surveyors north to organize a militia and attack Riel. Most English-speaking settlers ignored the call to arms, but some of Riel's fiercest opponents got ready to march on Fort Garry. Riel learned of their plans and took them prisoner before they could attack.

In the new year, the Red River committee voted to set up its own government, with twenty-five-year-old Riel as president. Riel made it clear that the area would join Canada only as an independent province, not a controlled-by-Ottawa territory. In March 1870, his new government charged one prisoner—a violent, bigoted newcomer from Ontario named Thomas Scott—with treason. Scott was found guilty and sentenced to death. Riel voted against the execution, but he lost. The death of Scott would plague Riel for the rest of his life.

In May, Parliament passed a bill to make the Red River Settlement Canada's newest province, Manitoba. Riel had won, but he had lost too. Troops were sent west to restore peace, but many of them from Ontario wanted revenge against the Métis and treated them terribly. Moreover, an amnesty, or pardon, promised to Riel and other leaders never came, and Ontario put up a $5,000 reward for Riel for killing Scott.

Riel was now a hunted man. He spent the next several years hiding out in the United States or Quebec, sneaking home for only a few days every now and then. Three times he was chosen as a member of Parliament from Manitoba, but each time he was unable to represent his people. After the November 1873 election, he did manage to slip into Ottawa and be sworn in as an MP before anyone recognized him. But by then there was a warrant out for his arrest, as well as a price on his head, so he didn't dare show up again.

In 1875, Ottawa pardoned all the Red River Rebellion leaders but Riel. He was ordered to stay out of Canada for five more years before getting amnesty. The fear of being killed and the pressure of hiding started to get to Riel, and he became very depressed.

In January 1876, a worried uncle brought him back from the United States to Montreal. Riel was safe there. Most French-Canadian Catholics saw him as a hero who'd been unfairly targeted by English-speaking Protestants from Ontario. But Riel wasn't safe from himself. He was very confused, was seeing things that weren't there and often couldn't stop shouting or crying. His uncle had him put in a mental hospital. He was released two years later.

Riel would spend the next six years in the midwestern United States, often living and working with Métis and Native people. Every now and then he would show signs of mental stress, but he went on with life and continued to dream of freedom for his people. In 1881, he married a beautiful twenty-year-old Métis woman, Marguerite Monet. A year later they had a son, Jean, and in 1883 a baby girl.

In 1884, a famous buffalo hunter and Métis leader named Gabriel Dumont travelled nearly 1,200 kilometres from the Saskatchewan River Valley to ask Riel to return to Canada. Dumont told him that the same thing that had happened in Manitoba was happening all over again farther west, and that the Métis and Plains Indians living there needed his help. Riel, an American citizen by then, packed up his family and headed home.

This fight for rights and land claims would be brief but bloody. Ottawa moved quickly to put down a new government set up by Dumont, with Riel as its political leader, and extra North West Mounted Police forces were sent to Regina. Riel didn't want any bloodshed, but Dumont and some Native warriors were fed up with waiting for Ottawa to listen to them. Forts were captured and battles fought at Duck Lake, Frog Lake and Fish Lake. Ottawa sent out more soldiers.

The final battle took place at Batoche in May 1885. Canadian forces led by Gen. Frederick Middleton were well armed and outnumbered Dumont's men five to one. As Dumont fought on, Riel prayed for his people, but it was soon clear the Métis had lost. Dumont managed to escape, but on May 15 Riel turned himself in to the victors.

Riel was taken under guard to Regina. There, in July, he was tried for treason. His lawyers from Montreal said he was insane and could not be held responsible for his actions, but Riel said he wasn't. He made a powerful speech defending his efforts on behalf of his people that left many people in the courtroom crying. In the end, though, the jury found him guilty.

Prime Minister Macdonald faced roars of protest from Quebec and calls for the death of Scott's murderer from Ontario. Riel's execution was put off twice. But on November 11, 1885, Macdonald decided Riel had to die. On November 16, a calm, prayerful Riel climbed the scaffold steps, spoke softly to the tearful priest who was there to comfort him and bent his head into the noose.

Manitoba's founder was dead. His body was sent by train to St. Boniface, and on December 12, a two-kilometre-long line of mourners gathered to bid him farewell.

# Mistahimaskwa
## (Big Bear)
### 1825?–1888

**M**OST DETAILS of Big Bear's early life have been lost to history. He was born in what's now southern Saskatchewan, most likely in 1825. His parents may have belonged to the Saulteaux nation, but he grew up with and lived as a Plains Cree. Over his lifetime, he had at least three wives and several children, including four sons.

Like most other Plains Cree and many Métis, he was a proud hunter who took part year after year in the massive buffalo hunt that was a vital part of the social structure and culture of his people. It was also at the heart of his people's survival. The buffalo provided them with food, clothing and shelter, and when more and more fur traders worked their way west, it also gave them a source of income. They used the money they got from selling pemmican (dried buffalo meat) and hides to buy things like tools, food, material, thread, needles and beads.

But the more buyers there were for buffalo products, the more the animals were hunted. And as settlers started arriving on the prairies in both Canada and the United States, the buffalo had less and less space to roam. By the 1870s, Big Bear could see that the buffalo herds were getting smaller each year, and he worried about what his people would do when they were gone. Other Natives began to make treaties with the Canadian government, agreeing to give up their vast hunting grounds in exchange for smaller, clearly defined territories, or reserves, and for an annual payment of money. The government also agreed to give Natives on reserves extra food supplies if they needed them.

But in 1876, Big Bear refused to make such a deal on behalf of the Plains Cree and Assiniboians who still hunted the buffalo. The way he saw it, they could take care of themselves as long as they could follow their traditional ways. He believed that the reserves weren't big enough to support the level of hunting, fishing and trapping Aboriginal people living on them would need to survive, and that much of the reserve land wasn't very good for farming. So he kept turning down treaty offers. He also refused to accept any gifts from government officials trying to convince him that he was making a mistake by not accepting their terms. He saw their gifts as bribes, and there was no way he was going to be bought off with a few kilograms of tea and tobacco.

Other Cree warriors were impressed with Big Bear's courageous attitude and wisdom, and they began to follow him, even though some of their chiefs had already signed treaties. They liked the way he spoke about how important it was for Natives to act together when dealing with the people who were taking over their land. But by 1882, Big Bear felt he had no choice but to sign a treaty. The buffalo herds were finally gone, and most of his people were starving. They desperately needed the food and money such a deal would bring.

Still, Big Bear knew that the money wouldn't go very far. The payments, to be made each year for as long as grass grew and water ran, amounted to twenty-five dollars for each chief, fifteen dollars for members of the band council and five dollars for every other person. As soon as people got that money, they went right to the Hudson's Bay Company posts and bought the food and supplies they needed. But without a chance to hunt and fish as they had in the past, they soon found themselves hungry and sick again, long before the next annual payments were due.

Big Bear hated what was happening to his people. He argued with government officials about how unfair the treaties were, and kept trying to get a better deal for his people. More warriors joined him, and by 1884 he had at least two thousand followers. In the summer of 1884, he and his followers arrived at Chief Poundmaker's reserve, near Battleford, Saskatchewan. There he held meetings to try to get other Cree chiefs to work with him to get one big reserve on good land on the North Saskatchewan River. But some of his warriors were frustrated by all the talking and negotiating. They wanted to face their people's enemies head-on if they didn't get what they wanted.

Big Bear knew that fighting the government officials and the newly formed North West Mounted Police (NWMP) could only bring disaster to his people. He paid close attention to what was happening with Gabriel Dumont and Louis Riel (see p. 227), who were demanding fairer treatment for their people not far away at Prince Albert. He hoped that they could get results without having to resort to fighting. Then he'd be able to show his warriors that tough words were more powerful weapons than guns. Sadly, those talks failed, and in March 1885 violence broke out at Duck Lake and the Northwest Rebellion had begun.

When news of the fighting there reached Big Bear's camp, other young warriors said the time had come for them to fight too. Big Bear tried to talk them out of planning any attacks, but they ignored him and started listening to other leaders, including one of Big Bear's sons, who were ready to start beating the war drums. On April 2, 1885, some of Big Bear's men attacked the settlement at Frog Lake. Nine settlers, including two priests, were killed, and the settlement was destroyed. A week and a half later, at least 250 warriors surrounded Fort Pitt and warned the twenty-five Mounties there that if the fifty or so people inside didn't leave the fort, they would all be slaughtered. Against such odds, NWMP Inspector Francis Dickens had no choice but to abandon the fort and move everyone to safety at Battleford.

After a large force of soldiers led by Gen. Frederick Middleton reached the area, it didn't take long for the rebellion to be put down. By the end of June, most of the fighting was over. Chief Poundmaker, who like Big Bear had tried to prevent the senseless killing, had surrendered earlier, but Big Bear hadn't been caught yet. However, on July 2, 1885, he suddenly appeared at Fort Carlton and turned himself in to an astonished NWMP officer on duty there. He and several of his men were taken to Regina and tried for treason. Even though he had tried to stop the fighting, and had helped save the lives of several prisoners, a jury found Big Bear guilty. But its members recommended that the judge show him mercy. He sentenced the once-powerful, proud Cree chief to three years in prison.

By then, Big Bear was getting old, and prison took a heavy toll on him. His health failed, and he was finally released a year early. While he was in prison, his people had moved to many different reserves, so he had no place to call home. He lived out his last days on Chief Poundmaker's reserve, dying there on January 17, 1888. Some Cree followers found the news of his death hard to believe. Maybe they didn't want to believe it. With Big Bear's passing, they could no longer deny that the cries, laughter and cheers of proud, fiercely independent buffalo hunters had finally been silenced on the western plains.

# Photo Credits

Alexander Mackenzie: National Archives C1348

Bishop François de Laval: Musée de l'Université Laval

Comte de Frontenac: Archives of Ontario S431

Étienne Brûlé: National Archives PAC C73635

George Vancouver: City of Vancouver Archives PORT.P.346.N.162

George-Étienne Cartier: National Archives PAC C6166

Henry Hudson: National Archives PAC C-2061

Jacques Cartier: National Archives PAC C11226

James Douglas: National Archives

Jean de Brébeuf: National Archives PAC C-1470

Jean Talon: Metropolitan Toronto Reference Library/
    J. Ross Robertson Collection T15467

Jeanne Mance: National Archives PAC C14360

John Cabot: National Archives PAC C-70249

John Graves Simcoe: National Archives PAC C-73667

Joseph Howe: National Archives C-7158

Josiah Henson: Metropolitan Toronto Public Library Collection

Laura Secord: National Archives/Estate Lorne K. Smith C-11053

Lord Selkirk: Toronto Reference Library

Louis Jolliet: National Archives PAC-C70269

Louis Riel: National Archives A498

Louis-Hippolyte LaFontaine: National Archives PAC C-5961

Louis-Joseph Papineau: National Archives

Kateri Tekakwitha: National Archives C003313

Marguerite Bourgeoys: Metropolitan Toronto Public Library Collection

Madeleine Jarret de Verchères: National Archives/ C.W. Jefferys C-10687

Martin Frobisher: Metro Toronto Reference Library/ J. Ross Robertson Collection T15484

Mistahimaskwa: National Archives PAC C-1873

Louis-Joseph de Montcalm: National Archives PAC C1457

Pierre-Esprit Radisson: National Archives C-15497

Pierre Le Moyne d'Iberville: National Archives/ C.W. Jefferys PAC C70248

René-Robert Cavelier de La Salle: National Archives PAC-C17560

Robert Baldwin: Metropolitan Toronto Reference Library/ J. Ross Robertson Collection T15006

Samuel de Champlain: Archives of Ontario A04587

Shawnadithit: Provincial Archives of Newfoundland & Labrador 906.043.99

Sieur de Maisonneuve: National Archives PA-32288

Sir Isaac Brock: Metropolitan Toronto Reference Library/ J. Ross Robertson Collection T15503

Sir John A. Macdonald: Toronto Reference Library T31118

William Lyon Mackenzie: Toronto Reference Library T31909

James Wolfe: National Archives C12248

# Index